Welcome to Umbria

3 | **Umbria Travel Guide** 2 0 2 5

Umbria Map

Umbria Travel Guide 2025: Your Ultimate Journey to Italy's Green Heart

Explore Assisi, Perugia, Spoleto, and Orvieto – Discover Umbria's Hidden Gems, Majestic Countryside, UNESCO Heritage Sites, Wine Roads, Cuisine and Insider Tips, Maps and Budget Stays

Kurt Becker

All rights reserved. Except for brief quotations included in reviews and their specific commercial uses permitted by copyright law, no part of this publication may be duplicated, distributed, or transmitted in any way without the permission of the publisher, including recording, photocopying, or other electronic means.

Copyright © Kurt Becker, 2025.

TABLE OF CONTENTS

TABLE OF CONTENTS 5
Chapter 1 11
Introduction 11
    Geography and Climate 17
    Terrain and Landscape 17
    Climate 17
    Culture and Customs 19
Chapter 2 22
Planning your trip 22
    Best Time to Visit 22
    Visa and Entry Requirements 32
    What to Pack 35
Chapter 3 39
Getting There 39
    By Air: 39
    By Train: 42

By Bus:..43

By Car:...45

Getting around Umbria..........................49

Public Transportation 49

Car Rentals...49

Driving Tips:..50

Walking and Cycling Tips......................50

Chapter 4 52
Top Attractions in Umbria 52

Assisi – Basilica of San Francesco..........52

Perugia – Rocca Paolina........................56

Gubbio – Palazzo dei Consoli..................59

Orvieto – Orvieto Cathedral (Duomo di Orvieto) 63

Spoleto – Rocca Albornoziana 66

Todi – Museo di Palazzo Buonaccorsi.....70

Foligno – Pinacoteca Civica (Civic Gallery) 73

Cascata delle Marmore (Marmore Falls) 77

Lake Trasimeno 81

Montefalco – Sagrantino Vineyards 85

Chapter 5 .... **90**

Accommodations **90**

Historic Hotels: 91

Modern Resorts 95

Bed and Breakfasts (B&Bs) 99

Agriturismi (Farm Stays) 103

Boutique Inns 107

Holiday Apartments/Villas 111

Guesthouses 115

Hostels 119

Chapter 6 .... **122**

Culinary Delights in Umbria **122**

Traditional Umbrian Cuisines................ 123

Dining Etiquette....................................... 129

Umbrian Wines and Wineries................ 132

Coffee Culture.. 135

Culinary Adventures and Cooking Classes 138

Chapter 7 ....**141**

Shopping in Umbria......................**141**

Souvenirs and Local Crafts.....................141

Markets and Bazaars 143

Unique Shopping Districts..................... 144

Chapter 8 .... **149**

Festivals and Events - Celebrating Umbrian's Rich Heritage................ **149**

Annual Celebrations............................... 149

Cultural Events....................................... 152

Special Occasions 154

Chapter 9 158
Road Trip from Umbria 158

Planning Your Road Trip 158

Road Trip Essentials 159

Roadside Discoveries 160

Accommodations on the Road 161

Day Trip Tips 161

Chapter 10 164
7-Day Umbria Itinerary 164

Day 1: Welcome to Umbria City 164

Day 2: Exploring Historical Sites 165

Day 3: Nature and Outdoor Activities ... 166

Day 4: Culinary Delights 167

Day 5: Relaxation and Leisure 168

Day 6: Local Art and Culture 169

Day 7: Farewell and Departure 169

Cooking Recipes 170

Chapter 11 173
Practical Tips for a Seamless Umbrian Experience 173

Safety and Emergency Information 173

Sustainable Travel Practices 176

Health and Medical Facilities in Umbria 177

Useful Italian Phrases for Your Trip to Umbria 178

Conclusion 182

Chapter 1

Introduction

Welcome to Umbria, a region nestled in the heart of Italy. Encompassing beautiful popular cities like Perugia, Assisi, Orvieto and Spoleto.

Umbria is a place where rolling hills adorned with olive groves and vineyards paint a picturesque landscape. This hidden gem often referred to as the "**Green Heart of Italy**," beckons travelers with its timeless allure, where every cobblestone whispers tales of ancient civilizations and each medieval town stands as a testimony to the region's rich history.

In writing this travel guide, I dive into my own memorable experiences in Umbria, a place surrounded by a landscape that seems to have been carefully crafted by the hands of both nature and history.

Verdant valleys give way to charming hilltop villages, each with its own unique character and story to tell.

It's a place where time slows down, allowing you to savor every moment, every flavor, and every breathtaking panorama. Umbria is not just a destination; it's an immersive experience that invites you to explore the essence of Italian culture and hospitality.

Whether you're wandering through the narrow streets of **Assisi,** the birthplace of **St. Francis,** or marveling at the medieval architecture of Perugia, every corner reveals a piece of Umbrian's captivating past. The art and history seamlessly blend with the rhythm of daily life, creating a tapestry that captivates the soul.

For those seeking a spiritual journey, Umbrian's spiritual centers, ancient churches, and sacred sites offer a serene haven for reflection.

As you stand before the **Basilica of Saint Francis** or walk through the sacred halls of the **Cathedral of Orvieto**, you'll feel a profound connection to centuries of devotion. But Umbria is not just a museum of history; it's a vibrant canvas of contemporary life.

The lively piazzas, bustling markets, and spirited festivals bring the region to life, inviting you to engage with the locals and partake in the authentic rhythm of Umbrian culture. Indulge in the warmth of the people, the laughter echoing through the vineyards, and the aromatic flavors that define the region's delectable cuisine.

Speaking of cuisine, Umbria is a haven for food enthusiasts. From truffle-infused delicacies to hearty local dishes, every meal is a celebration of fresh, locally sourced ingredients. Sip on robust wines from the region's vineyards, where each glass tells a story of the sun-drenched hills and the passion of the winemakers.

This travel guide is your key to unlocking the secrets of Umbria, providing a roadmap to navigate the wonders that await you. Join us on a journey through time, taste, and tradition, as we unveil the hidden treasures, share insider tips, and guide you to the most enchanting corners of this captivating region. Let Umbria weave its spell around you, and may your exploration be filled with discovery, wonder, and the joy of experiencing la dolce vita in its purest form.

Buon viaggio – have a wonderful journey!

Why This Guide is perfect for the 2025 Season

Firstly, this guide is meticulously up to date, offering the latest information on travel regulations, safety protocols, and local guidelines, ensuring that visitors are well-informed and can navigate their journey with confidence and ease.

One of its standout features is its in-depth coverage of side attractions. In **2025**, travelers seek not only the main highlights but also the hidden gems that make a destination truly memorable.

This guide's comprehensive insights into lesser-known attractions promise a well-rounded and authentic experience for those eager to delve deeper into Umbrian's rich tapestry.

The section on foods is a culinary odyssey, introducing visitors to the diverse and delectable world of Umbrian cuisine. With recommendations on traditional dishes, local eateries, and dining etiquette, this guide ensures that every meal becomes a celebration of the region's flavors and culinary traditions.

Weather and climate information is crucial for trip planning. The guide provides a thorough overview, helping visitors pack appropriately and makes the most of their time in Umbria, whether enjoying the warm summer sun or embracing the crisp air of the cooler seasons. Understanding customs and cultural nuances is pivotal for respectful travel.

This guide goes beyond the usual attractions, offering insights into local customs, traditions, and social etiquette. This cultural immersion enhances the travel experience, fostering a deeper connection between visitors and the vibrant Umbrian way of life.

To facilitate communication, the guide includes a handy section on common Italian phrases frequently used by visitors. This linguistic aid empowers travelers to engage with locals, fostering a sense of camaraderie and making their journey more enriching.

Beyond being a mere informational resource, this guide serves as a true companion.

Its well-crafted itineraries, practical tips, and user-friendly format make it an indispensable tool for travelers navigating the enchanting landscapes of Umbria.

Whether exploring historic sites, savoring local delicacies, or navigating public transportation, the guide ensures that every moment of the journey is guided by knowledge and insight.

In essence, this Travel Guide goes beyond the conventional, offering a dynamic and immersive experience that aligns perfectly with the desires and expectations of contemporary travelers.

Geography and Climate

Umbria, situated in central Italy, is characterized by diverse geography and a temperate climate. The region is landlocked and largely mountainous, with the Apennine Mountains dominating its eastern border. The landscape is adorned with rolling hills, lush valleys, and picturesque plains, creating a captivating and varied terrain.

Terrain and Landscape

Lake Trasimeno, one of Italy's largest lakes, lies to the west of Umbria, adding to the region's natural beauty. The Tiber River, flowing through the eastern part of Umbria, contributes to the fertile plains and provides water to the region.

Climate

Umbria experiences a Mediterranean climate, meaning it has hot, dry summers and cool, wet winters. Here is a breakdown of the seasons:

1. Spring (March to May): Spring is a delightful season with blooming flowers, lush greenery, and milder temperatures. It's an excellent time for outdoor activities, exploring the countryside, and witnessing the awakening of nature. Average temperature ranges from 10°C to 20°C (50°F to 68°F).

2. Summer (June to August): Summer brings warm and dry weather, making it the peak tourist season. It's ideal for enjoying outdoor festivals, exploring historic sites, and relaxing by the lakes. Temperature ranges from 20°C to 35° (68°F to 95°F). Be prepared for higher temperatures, especially in July and August.

3. Autumn (September to November): Autumn offers a pleasant transition from summer to winter.

The landscape transforms into warm hues, and the weather remains mild. It's a great time for wine tours, truffle hunting, and enjoying the harvest season. Temperature ranges from 10°C to 20°C (50°F to 68°F).

4. Winter (December to February): Winters in Umbria are cool, and higher elevations may experience snowfall. It's a quieter period for tourism, but it offers a unique charm, especially during the holiday season.

Winter is suitable for exploring historic towns, enjoying regional winter dishes, and experiencing local traditions. Temperature ranges from 0°C to 15°C degrees Celsius (32°F to 59°F).

Understanding the seasonal variations in Umbria allow you to plan your visit based on personal preferences and the type of experience you seek.

Whether enjoying the vibrant colors of spring, the warmth of summer, the harvest festivities of autumn, or the tranquility of winter, Umbria offers a captivating experience throughout the year.

Culture and Customs

Umbria, situated in central Italy, boasts a rich tapestry of culture and customs that reflect its historical significance and deep-rooted traditions. Here are some key aspects of Umbrian culture and customs:

Spirituality and Festivals: Umbria is renowned for its spiritual heritage, particularly as the birthplace of St. Francis of Assisi. Religious festivals and processions are significant events in the region, drawing pilgrims and visitors from around the world.

Art and Craftsmanship: The artistic heritage of Umbria is evident in its medieval towns adorned with frescoes, sculptures, and architectural marvels. The region is also known for its traditional handicrafts, including ceramics, textiles, and woodworking.

Culinary Traditions: Umbrian cuisine is characterized by its farm-to-table philosophy, with dishes highlighting local produce such as olive oil, truffles, and cured meats. Wine culture thrives in Umbria, with vineyards producing quality wines like Sagrantino di Montefalco and Orvieto Classico.

Community Engagement: Umbrian communities are known for their close-knit nature and strong social connections. Visitors often find themselves welcomed into local festivities, markets, and communal celebrations, where they can experience the warmth and hospitality of the region.

Natural Connection: Many Umbrian maintain a close connection to the land, engaging in agriculture and embracing a slower, rural lifestyle. The region's landscapes, including olive groves, vineyards, and picturesque countryside, reflect this deep-rooted connection to nature.

Understanding Umbrian's culture and customs will enhance your travel experience, enhancing you to adapt with the locals and enroll yourself in the city and diverse way of life.

Chapter 2

Planning your trip

Best Time to Visit

The best time to visit Umbria depends on your preferences for weather, activities, and the type of experience you seek. Here's a breakdown of the seasons to help you decide when to plan your visit:

Spring, spanning from March to May, is a delightful period for visitors in Umbria. Here are some reasons why spring is an excellent time to explore the region:

1. Mild Weather: During spring, Umbria experiences mild temperatures ranging from 10 to 20 degrees Celsius (50 to 68 degrees Fahrenheit). The weather is pleasant for outdoor activities and exploration.

2. Blooming Nature: Spring brings the countryside to life with vibrant colors as flowers bloom and trees blossom.

The landscape is a picturesque tapestry of greenery and floral beauty, making it ideal for nature walks and scenic drives.

3. Cultural Festivals: Spring marks the beginning of several cultural festivals and events in Umbria. From religious celebrations to music festivals and art exhibitions, there are numerous opportunities to immerse you in the region's rich cultural heritage.

4. Outdoor Activities: With the mild weather, spring is perfect for outdoor adventures such as hiking, cycling, and picnicking. Umbrian's rolling hills, meandering trails, and scenic vistas provide the backdrop for unforgettable outdoor experiences.

5. Less Crowded: Compared to the peak summer season, spring sees fewer tourists, allowing visitors to enjoy popular attractions and landmarks without the crowds. It's an excellent time to explore charming towns, visit historic sites, and interact with locals.

6. Gastronomic Delights: Spring brings a bounty of fresh produce to Umbrian's markets and restaurants. Visitors can indulge in seasonal delicacies, including wild asparagus, artichokes, and fava beans, as well as sample local cheeses, cured meats, and olive oil.

Overall, spring offers a perfect balance of pleasant weather, natural beauty, cultural events, and culinary delights, making it an ideal time for visitors to experience the charm and allure of Umbria.

The summer period in Umbria, spanning from June to August, offers a vibrant and lively atmosphere for visitors. Here are some key aspects to consider if you plan to visit Umbria during the summer:

1. Warm and Sunny Weather: Summer brings warm to hot temperatures, ranging from 20 to 35 degrees Celsius (68 to 95 degrees Fahrenheit). The region enjoys long sunny days, making it an ideal time for outdoor activities and exploration.

2. Peak Tourist Season: Summer is the peak tourist season in Umbria, attracting visitors from around the world. Popular attractions, historic sites, and cultural events may be busier during this period.

It's advisable to plan and book accommodations in advance.

3. Outdoor Festivals and Events: The summer season in Umbria is marked by a plethora of outdoor festivals, music events, and cultural celebrations.

The Umbria Jazz Festival in Perugia is a highlight, attracting jazz enthusiasts and performers.

4. Lake and Water Activities: Umbrian's Lake Trasimeno, one of Italy's largest lakes, becomes a popular destination during the summer. Visitors can enjoy water activities such as swimming, sailing, and kayaking or relax on the lake's shores.

5. Historic Towns and Hilltop Villages: Explore charming historic towns and hilltop villages in the cooler parts of the day, as temperatures can be higher during the midday hours. Enjoy the local architecture, cultural sites, and vibrant street life.

6. Al Fresco Dining: Take advantage of the warm evenings for al fresco dining in the region's picturesque squares and outdoor restaurants. Enjoy traditional Umbrian cuisine paired with local wines.

7. Lively Atmosphere: The summer months bring a lively and festive atmosphere to Umbria. Street markets, open-air concerts, and cultural events create a vibrant ambiance, providing a rich cultural experience for visitors.

While summer in Umbria offers an energetic and bustling environment, it's essential to plan for the higher temperatures and the increased number of tourists. If you enjoy vibrant festivals, warm weather, and a lively atmosphere, summer can be an excellent time to visit this beautiful region in central Italy.

Autumn, spanning from September to November, offers a beautiful and tranquil time for visitors to explore Umbria. Here are some reasons why autumn is a wonderful period to visit this picturesque region:

1. Mild Weather: Umbria experiences mild temperatures during autumn, ranging from 10 to 20 degrees Celsius (50 to 68 degrees Fahrenheit). The weather is comfortable for outdoor activities and sightseeing, without the intense heat of summer or the cold of winter.

2. Vibrant Foliage: Autumn brings a stunning display of colors to Umbrian's countryside as the leaves change hues. The hillsides and vineyards are ablaze with shades of red, orange, and gold, creating a breathtaking backdrop for exploration and photography.

3. Harvest Season: Autumn is the harvest season in Umbria, offering visitors the opportunity to experience the region's agricultural traditions.

Join in grape and olive harvests, visit local farms and vineyards, and sample fresh produce at farmers' markets.

4. Wine Festivals: Autumn is synonymous with wine festivals in Umbria, celebrating the grape harvest and the region's winemaking heritage. Visitors can participate in wine tastings, vineyard tours, and wine-pairing dinners, experiencing the rich flavors of Umbrian wines.

5. Truffle Season: Umbria is renowned for its truffles, and autumn marks the beginning of the truffle season. Visitors can embark on truffle hunts with trained dogs, visit truffle markets, and savor gourmet dishes featuring this prized delicacy.

6. Cultural Events: Autumn is a time for cultural events and festivals throughout Umbria. From music concerts and art exhibitions to food festivals and traditional celebrations, there are numerous opportunities to immerse you in the region's rich cultural heritage.

7. Scenic Drives and Hiking Trails: Explore Umbrian's scenic countryside and picturesque villages on leisurely drives or hikes. The cooler temperatures and clear skies make autumn ideal for outdoor exploration, offering breathtaking vistas of rolling hills and medieval towns.

Overall, autumn in Umbria offers a serene and enchanting experience, with its vibrant colors, culinary delights, and cultural festivities. Whether you're a nature enthusiast, a food lover, or a culture seeker, Umbrian's autumn landscape and charm are sure to captivate visitors.

Winter, spanning from December to February, provides a unique and tranquil experience for visitors to Umbria. Here are some aspects to note if you plan to visit during the winter months:

1. Cooler Temperatures: Winter in Umbria brings cooler temperatures, ranging from 0 to 15 degrees Celsius (32 to 59 degrees Fahrenheit).

While some areas may experience snowfall, especially at higher elevations, the overall climate is milder compared to Northern Europe.

2. Holiday Festivities: December is a festive time in Umbria, marked by Christmas and New Year's celebrations. Towns and cities are adorned with festive decorations, and holiday markets offer a charming atmosphere for visitors to enjoy seasonal treats and shop for unique gifts.

3. Culinary Delights: Winter is an excellent time to indulge in Umbrian's hearty and comforting winter cuisine. Warm up with traditional dishes such as Ribollita (a Tuscan soup), lentil stew, and truffle-infused specialties. Local restaurants offer seasonal menus featuring winter flavors.

4. Winter Sports: If you enjoy winter sports, certain areas in the Apennine Mountains offer opportunities for skiing and snowboarding. Mount Subasio, near Assisi, is one such location where visitors can enjoy winter activities and scenic landscapes.

5. Historical and Cultural Exploration: Explore Umbrian's historic towns and cultural sites without the crowds that often accompany the peak tourist seasons.

Museums, churches, and medieval villages take on a serene ambiance, allowing for a more intimate and reflective experience.

6. Local Traditions: Experience local winter traditions and festivities that may include processions, nativity scenes, and historical reenactments. These events provide insight into Umbrian's rich cultural heritage and traditions during the winter months.

7. Wine Tasting by the Fireplace: Cozy up in local wineries and wine bars that offer tastings by the fireplace. You should sample regional wines, including robust reds like Sagrantino di Montefalco, while enjoying the warmth and ambiance of the winter season.

While winter in Umbria may not be characterized by extreme cold, it offers a quieter and more contemplative atmosphere, allowing visitors to appreciate the region's cultural, culinary, and natural beauty at a more relaxed pace.

Consider your preferences for weather and the type of activities you want to engage in. If you enjoy vibrant festivals and warm weather, summer might be ideal. To have a relaxed and cultural experience, spring and autumn offer pleasant temperatures and unique events. Winter, with its festive ambiance, is perfect for those seeking a quieter, atmospheric visit.

Visa and Entry Requirements

Umbria is a region in Italy, and Italy is a member of the Schengen Area. If you're planning to visit Umbria for tourism, you will need to consider the general visa and entry requirements for the Schengen Area.

However, please note that immigration policies can change, and it's essential to verify the latest information with the relevant authorities or the official website of the Italian government.

Here are some general guidelines regarding visa and entry requirements:

1. Schengen Area:

Italy, including Umbria, is part of the Schengen Area. If you are a citizen of a Schengen member country, you typically do not need a visa for short stays (up to 90 days within a 180-day period).

2. Non-Schengen Countries:

If you are a citizen of a non-Schengen country, you may need a Schengen visa for short visits. Check with the Italian consulate or embassy in your country to determine the specific requirements and application procedures.

3. Visa-Free Countries:

Citizens of certain countries, even those outside the Schengen Area, may be exempt from a visa requirement for short visits. This depends on bilateral agreements and diplomatic relations. Check from the relevant authorities for the latest information.

4. Longer Stays:

If you plan to stay in Umbria for longer than 90 days (for work, study, or other purposes), you may need a national visa or residence permit. These usually require additional documentation and an application process.

5. Passport Validity:

You should ensure that your passport is valid for at least three months beyond your intended departure date from the Schengen Area.

6. Documentation:

When entering Umbria, have essential travel documents, including a valid passport, visa (if required), and any supporting documentation such as travel insurance, accommodation details, and proof of sufficient funds.

7. Dual Nationalities:

If you have dual nationality, be aware that entry requirements may vary depending on the passport you use. Check from the relevant authorities for guidance.

Check the latest visa requirements and entry regulations from the Italian consulate or embassy in your home country or visit the official website of the Italian government. Additionally, keep an eye on any travel advisories issued by your government regarding travel to Italy.

Italian Government website: https://www.governo.it/en

Understanding and adhering to the visa and entry requirements will ensure a smooth arrival in Umbria and a hassle-free start to your exploration through.

What to Pack

Packing for your trip to Umbria requires consideration of the cultural norms, weather conditions, and cultural experiences. Here's a comprehensive packing list for your journey to Umbria:

1. Clothing:

  - Lightweight, breathable clothing for warmer period.

  - Layered clothing for cooler seasons and evenings.

  - Comfortable walking shoes for exploring towns and countryside.

  - Closed-toe shoes for hiking and outdoor activities.

  - Swimsuit for visiting lakes or swimming pools in the summer.

  - Rain jackets or umbrella for unexpected showers.

2. Accessories:

- Sun hat or cap to shield from the sun.

- Sunglasses to protect your eyes from UV rays.

- Scarf /shawl for cooler evenings.

- Daypack or tote bag for carrying essentials during outings.

- Travel adapter and chargers for electronic device.

3. Health and Personal Care:

- Prescription medications and necessary medical supplies.

- Sunscreen with high SPF for sun protection.

- Insect repellent, especially in rural areas.

- Basic first-aid kit including bandages, antiseptic wipes, and pain relievers.

- Hand sanitizer or sanitizing wipes for hygiene on the go

4. Travel Documents:

- Valid passport with at least six months validity

- Visa (if required) with travel insurance documents

- Printed copies of accommodation reservations and travel itinerary

- Emergency contact information and copies of important documents.

5. Technology and Gadgets:

- Camera or Smartphone for capturing memories

- Portable power bank to recharge devices on the go

- Travel guidebooks or maps for navigation and trip planning

- Language translation app or phrasebook for communication

7. Cultural Considerations:

- Modest clothing for visiting churches and religious places

- Respectful attire for dining at upscale restaurants or attending cultural events

- Language guide or basic Italian phrases for communication with locals

6. Miscellaneous Items:

- Reusable water bottle to stay hydrated

- Snacks for energy during excursions and long drives

- Travel-sized toiletries and personal hygiene products

- Foldable travel umbrella for unexpected rain showers

- Lightweight, foldable tote bag for shopping and souvenirs

By packing wisely and considering the activities and weather conditions you'll encounter in Umbria, you'll ensure a comfortable and enjoyable travel experience in this beautiful region of Italy.

Chapter 3

Getting There

Umbria is a region in central Italy, known for its picturesque landscapes, historic towns, and cultural attractions. To get to Umbria, you can typically choose between various transportation options depending on your starting point. Here are some general guidelines:

By Air:

San Francesco d'Assisi – Umbria International Airport (PEG)

Address: Via dell'Aeroporto, snc, 06134 Perugia PG, Italy

Location: 16 kilometers (10 miles) east of Perugia

Phone number: +39 075 592141
Website: http://www.airport.umbria.it/

Opening hours: 24/7

The airport is situated in the municipality of Sant'Egidio, which is why it is also known as Perugia Sant'Egidio Airport.

It serves as the main airport for the Umbria region and is named after Saint Francis of Assisi, a well-known Italian saint.

If you are traveling to Perugia or other parts of Umbria, this airport provides a convenient gateway to the region. You can reach Perugia and other towns in Umbria from the airport by using taxis, car rentals, or other local transportation options.

Guidelines to fly to Perugia

1. Fly directly to Perugia:

  - The San Francesco d'Assisi – Umbria International Airport (PEG) in Perugia is the main airport in Umbria.

Book a Flight:

  - Search for flights to the San Francesco d'Assisi – Umbria International Airport (PEG).

Arriving at San Francesco d'Assisi – Umbria International Airport (PEG):

- If your destination is Perugia or other parts of Umbria, landing at PEG is the most convenient option.

- The airport is relatively small, and you can find car rental services, taxis, and shuttle services at the airport for onward transportation.

- You can take a direct flight to Perugia from some European cities or connect through major Italian airports.

2. Fly to Rome or Florence:

Alternatively, you can check flights to major airports in Rome or Florence and then plan to travel to Umbria by train, bus, or car.

- If there are no direct flights to Perugia, you can fly into Rome (Fiumicino or Ciampino airports) or Florence (Peretola Airport) and then take a train or bus to Umbria.

By Train:

Trenitalia

Location: Headquarters of Ferrovie dello Stato Italiane in Rome, Italy.

Website: https://www.trenitalia.com/en.html

Phone number +39 06 5210550

Active Time: 7am-11:59pm.

Trenitalia is the primary train operator in Italy which is a subsidiary of **Ferrovie dello Stato Italiane**

And partly owned by the Italian government, the company and partly from private investors group

1. Train from Rome or Florence:

- You can take a train from Rome or Florence to major Umbrian cities like Perugia, Assisi, or Terni.

- The train journey offers beautiful views of the Italian countryside.

By Bus:

Traveling to Umbria by bus is a viable option, especially if you're looking for cost-effective transportation. Here are some general guidelines for traveling to Umbria by bus:

1. Long-Distance Buses:

 - Long-distance bus services connect major Italian cities, and some international services may also be available. Companies like FlixBus and other regional operators offer routes to cities in Umbria.

2. Bus Stations:

 - Umbria has various bus stations in its major cities. Perugia, the capital of Umbria, has a central bus station called Piazzale Umbria Jazz, which serves as a hub for regional and long-distance buses.

3. Regional and Local Buses:

 - Once you arrive in Umbria, local and regional buses can take you to different towns and attractions within the region. These buses are an excellent way to explore the smaller towns and picturesque landscapes.

4. Bus Routes to Umbria:

 - The specific bus routes to Umbria may vary depending on your starting point. Major cities in Italy, such as Rome and Florence, are well-connected to Umbria by bus.

5. Ticketing and Reservations:

 - Bus tickets can be purchased online or at the bus station. It's advisable to check the schedule and book tickets in advance, especially during peak travel times.

6. Travel Time:

 - Traveling by bus to Umbria may take longer than other modes of transportation.

 Consider the duration of your journey when planning your itinerary.

7. Connections to Airports:

 - Buses often connect cities in Umbria to nearby airports. For example, you can take a bus from

Perugia to Perugia San Francesco d'Assisi – Umbria International Airport.

8. Bus Operators:

- Popular bus operators in Italy, such as FlixBus, Baltour, and Marino, may offer services to Umbria. Check their websites for routes, schedules, and ticket information.

Remember to check the current bus schedules, routes, and availability based on your travel dates. Bus travel can be a convenient and economical option, particularly if you prefer a more budget-friendly means of transportation.

By Car:

Renting a Car:

Renting a car is a convenient and popular option for traveling to Umbria, especially if you want the flexibility to explore the region at your own pace. Here are some key considerations and steps to keep in mind when renting a car for your trip to Umbria:

1. Choose a Rental Car Company:

- Research and select a reputable car rental company. Major international companies, as well as local providers, may have offices at airports and in city centers.

2. Booking in Advance:

- It's advisable to book your rental car in advance, especially if you are traveling during peak seasons. This ensures availability and may also lead to cost savings.

3. Pickup and Drop-Off Locations:

- Select convenient pickup and drop-off locations based on your itinerary. Airports, train stations, and city centers are common rental car pickup points.

4. Driving License:

- Ensure that you have a valid driver's license. International visitors may need an International Driving Permit (IDP) in addition to their regular license. Check the specific requirements with the Rental Company and local authorities.

5. Age Requirements:

- Check the minimum age requirements for renting a car. In Italy, drivers are typically required to be at least 18 or 21 years old, depending on the rental company.

6. Car Insurance:

- Consider purchasing comprehensive insurance coverage for your rental car.

This may include Collision Damage Waiver (CDW), Theft Protection (TP), and liability coverage. Verify the coverage details with the rental company.

7. Road Rules and Regulations:

- Familiarize yourself with the road rules and regulations in Italy. This includes speed limits, traffic signs, and driving on the right side of the road.

8. Fuel Policy:

- Understand the fuel policy of the rental company. Some companies provide a full tank of gas and expect you to return the car with a full tank, while others may operate on a different policy.

9. Navigation and GPS:

- Consider renting a car with built-in GPS or bring your own navigation device. This is especially useful for exploring Umbrian's picturesque countryside and smaller towns.

10. Parking:

- Be aware of parking regulations in towns and cities. Some areas may have restricted zones, and parking fees may apply.

11. Toll Roads:

- Umbria has well-maintained highways, and you may encounter toll roads. Keep some cash (Euros) for toll payments.

Renting a car provides the freedom to explore Umbrian's charming towns, scenic landscapes, and off-the-beaten-path attractions. Plan your route, enjoy the flexibility, and make the most of your road trip through this beautiful region in central Italy.

Getting around Umbria

Exploring the enchanting region of Umbria is a joy, and fortunately, there are diverse transportation options to make your journey seamless.

Public Transportation

Buses: Umbria boasts an extensive regional bus network connecting major towns and cities. Local buses are a cost-effective means of transportation, offering scenic routes through the picturesque landscapes. Timetables can be obtained at bus stations or online.

Trains: The regional train network provides efficient connections between Umbrian towns. Traveling by train offers a comfortable and scenic experience, allowing you to relax and enjoy the countryside views.

Car Rentals

Renting a car in Umbria provides the utmost flexibility, allowing you to explore hidden gems and remote villages at your pace. Major international and local car rental companies have offices at airports and in city centers.

Driving Tips:

- Right side of the road is the driving side of Italy.

- You should get familiar with local road signs and speed limits.

- Parking is available in towns, but be aware of restricted zones and fees.

Walking and Cycling Tips

Umbrian's charming towns and countryside are best explored on foot or by bicycle.

Many towns have pedestrian-friendly zones, and cycling through vineyards and olive groves is a delightful way to experience the region's beauty.

Walking Tours: Guided walking tours are available in cities like Perugia and Assisi, providing insights into the rich history and culture of Umbria.

San Francesco d'Assisi" (PEG) airport in Perugia

Chapter 4

Top Attractions in Umbria

Assisi – Basilica of San Francesco

Location: Piazza San Francesco, 2, 06081 Assisi PG, Italy

Phone Number: +39 075 819001

Website: http://www.sanfrancescoassisi.org/)

Opening Hours:

- April to September: 6:00 AM to 7:00 PM (last admission at 6:45 PM)

- October to March: 6:30 AM to 6:00 PM (last admission at 5:45 PM)

Entry Fee:

- Basilica Upper Church: €4

- Basilica Lower Church: €3

- Crypt of St. Francis: €2

History:

- The Basilica of San Francesco is a UNESCO World Heritage Site and one of the most important pilgrimage sites in Italy.

- Constructed between 1228 and 1253, the basilica is dedicated to St. Francis of Assisi, the patron saint of Italy, and founder of the Franciscan Order.

- The basilica is comprised of the Upper Church, built in Gothic style, and the Lower Church, featuring Romanesque architecture.

Attractions:

1. Upper Church:

  - Admire the stunning frescoes by renowned artists such as Giotto, Cimabue, and Simone Martini, depicting scenes from the life of St. Francis.

  - Explore the ornate Gothic architecture and the rose window, symbolizing the divine light.

2. Lower Church:

  - Visit the Lower Church, adorned with beautiful frescoes and intricate decorations.

  - Pay homage at the tomb of St. Francis, located in the crypt beneath the main altar.

3. Crypt of St. Francis:

  - Descend into the crypt to see the simple stone sarcophagus containing the remains of St. Francis.

- Experience the peaceful atmosphere of the crypt, where pilgrims from around the world come to pay their respects.

Things to Do:

- Attend a guided tour to gain deeper insights into the life and teachings of St. Francis and the artistic masterpieces within the basilica.

- Participate in Mass or religious services held regularly in the basilica.

- Take time to reflect and find inner peace in the serene surroundings of the basilica and its courtyards.

Visiting the Basilica of San Francesco is a profound spiritual and cultural experience, offering visitors a glimpse into the life and legacy of St. Francis and the artistic treasures of medieval Italy.

Perugia – Rocca Paolina

Location: Piazza Italia, 16, 06121 Perugia PG, Italy

Phone Number: +39 075 5722771

Website: https://www.comune.perugia.it/

Opening Hours:

- Monday to Sunday: 10:00 AM to 7:00 PM

Entry Fee:

- Standard: €5

- Reduced (for children aged 6-14, seniors over 65, and groups): €3

History:

- Rocca Paolina is a fortress that stands atop the ruins of the ancient city of Perugia, destroyed in 1540 by Pope Paul III.

- The fortress was designed by Antonio da Sangallo the Younger as a symbol of papal power and control over the rebellious city.

- The construction of the fortress involved demolishing a significant portion of the city, leading to the creation of a vast underground city.

Attractions:

1. Piazza Italia and the Viewpoint:

 - Admire the panoramic views of Perugia and the surrounding countryside from Piazza Italia, the square in front of Rocca Paolina.

2. The Underground City:

- Explore the fascinating underground passages and rooms that once formed the heart of the destroyed city.

- Visit the excavated rooms and discover remnants of houses, streets, and wells.

3. Temporary Exhibitions:

- Check for temporary exhibitions and events hosted within Rocca Paolina, featuring contemporary art and cultural displays.

Things to Do:

- Take a guided tour to gain insights into the history and significance of Rocca Paolina and the underground city.

- Attend cultural events, concerts, or art exhibitions that may be happening within the fortress.

- Enjoy a leisurely stroll in Piazza Italia and soak in the atmosphere of this historic setting.

Visiting Rocca Paolina offers a unique opportunity to witness the layers of history that shaped Perugia and explore the contrast between the medieval ruins and the vibrant city that emerged above ground.

Gubbio – Palazzo dei Consoli

Location: Piazza Grande, 06024 Gubbio PG, Italy

Phone Number: +39 075 9224931

Website: [Palazzo dei Consoli] http://www.gubbio-italy.org/

Opening Hours:

- Monday to Sunday: 10:00 AM to 1:00 PM, 3:00 PM to 7:00 PM

Entry Fee:

- Regular: €5

- Reduced (students and seniors): €3

- Free for children below 18 and disabled visitors

History:

- Palazzo dei Consoli is an iconic medieval palace located in the heart of Gubbio's historic center.

- Constructed in the early 14th century, the palace served as the seat of the local government and housed the offices of the city's governors.

- The palace features a distinctive Gothic design and served as a symbol of the city's power and prosperity during the middle Ages.

Attractions:

1. Museum of Gubbio:

- Explore the Museum of Gubbio located within Palazzo dei Consoli, showcasing a rich collection of archaeological finds, artifacts, and artworks spanning Gubbio's history.

- Highlights include prehistoric pottery, Roman artifacts, and medieval sculptures.

2. Eugubine Tablets:

- Admire the famous Eugubine Tablets, a set of seven bronze inscriptions dating back to the 3rd century BCE.

- The tablets contain one of the longest surviving texts in the ancient Umbrian language and provide valuable insights into the region's ancient culture and language.

Things to Do:

- Take a guided tour of Palazzo dei Consoli and the Museum of Gubbio to learn about the city's history, art, and culture.

- Explore the museum's various exhibitions, including displays of Roman and medieval artifacts, religious art, and historical documents.

- Enjoy panoramic views of Gubbio and the surrounding countryside from the terrace of Palazzo dei Consoli.

Visiting Palazzo dei Consoli offers a unique opportunity to delve into the rich history and cultural heritage of Gubbio while marveling at its magnificent architecture and artistic treasures.

Orvieto – Orvieto Cathedral (Duomo di Orvieto)

Location: Piazza Duomo, 26, 05018 Orvieto TR, Italy

Phone Number: +39 0763 342694

Website: http://www.opsm.it/

Opening Hours:

- Monday to Saturday: 10:00 AM to 5:00 PM

- Sunday: 12:30 PM to 5:00 PM

Entry Fee:

- Cathedral: €4

- Chapel of San Brizio: €3

History:

- Orvieto Cathedral, a masterpiece of Italian Gothic architecture, was constructed between 1290 and 1607.

- The cathedral was built to house the relic of the Corporal of Bolsena, a Eucharistic miracle that occurred in nearby Bolsena in the 13th century.

- The façade of the cathedral is adorned with intricate sculptures and mosaics, depicting scenes from the Old and New Testaments.

Attractions:

1. Façade and Exterior:

  - Marvel at the stunning façade of Orvieto Cathedral, featuring golden mosaics, sculptures, and intricate decorations.

- Admire the rose window and the statues of prophets and apostles adorning the exterior of the cathedral.

2. Interior and Chapel of San Brizio:

- Step inside the cathedral to explore its breathtaking interior, adorned with frescoes, stained glass windows, and ornate decorations.

- Visit the Chapel of San Brizio to admire Luca Signorelli's masterpiece, "The Last Judgment," a monumental fresco covering the entire chapel ceiling.

Things to Do:

- Take a guided tour of Orvieto Cathedral to learn about its history, architecture, and artistic significance.

- Attend a Mass or religious service to experience the cathedral's spiritual atmosphere and hear the beautiful organ music.

- Climb the bell tower for panoramic views of Orvieto and the surrounding Umbrian countryside.

Visiting Orvieto Cathedral offers a profound cultural and spiritual experience, allowing visitors to appreciate the beauty and artistry of one of Italy's most magnificent cathedrals.

Spoleto – Rocca Albornoziana

Location: Piazza Della Libertà, 06049 Spoleto PG, Italy

Phone Number: +39 0743 220066

Website: http://www.comunespoleto.gov.it/

Opening Hours:

- Tuesday to Sunday: 10:00 AM to 7:00 PM

- Closed on Mondays

Entry Fee:

- Regular: €5

- Reduced (students and seniors): €3

- Free for children below 18 and disabled visitors

History:

- Rocca Albornoziana is a medieval fortress built by the Spanish cardinal Egidio Albornoz in the 14th century.

- The fortress served as a military stronghold and residence for papal legates during the period of papal rule over Spoleto.

- Rocca Albornoziana played a strategic role in controlling the surrounding territory and defending the city from external threats.

Attractions:

1. Fortress Walls and Towers:

- Explore the impressive walls and towers of Rocca Albornoziana, offering panoramic views of Spoleto and the surrounding countryside.

- Walk along the ramparts and enjoy breathtaking vistas of the Umbrian landscape.

2. Courtyard and Inner Courtyards:

- Wander through the spacious courtyard of the fortress, surrounded by medieval buildings and structures.

- Discover the inner courtyards, featuring archaeological finds and exhibits related to the history of Spoleto.

Things to Do:

- Take a guided tour of Rocca Albornoziana to learn about its history, architecture, and military significance.

- Visit the museum housed within the fortress, showcasing artifacts, weapons, and medieval art.

- Attend cultural events and exhibitions held at Rocca Albornoziana, including concerts, theater performances, and art installations.

Exploring Rocca Albornoziana offers a captivating journey through Spoleto's medieval history and provides stunning views of the city and its surroundings.

Todi – Museo di Palazzo Buonaccorsi

Location: Piazza del Popolo, 06059 Todi PG, Italy

Phone Number: +39 075 8946626

Website: https://www.comune.todi.pg.it/

Opening Hours:

- Tuesday to Sunday: 10:00 AM to 1:00 PM, 3:00 PM to 7:00 PM

- Closed on Mondays

Entry Fee:

- Regular: €5

- Reduced (students and seniors): €3

- Free for children below 18 and disabled visitors

History:

- Museo di Palazzo Buonaccorsi is housed in the historic Palazzo Buonaccorsi, a Renaissance palace dating back to the 16th century.

- The palace was originally built by the Buonaccorsi family, prominent nobles of Todi, and served as their residence and administrative center.

- Today, Museo di Palazzo Buonaccorsi showcases a rich collection of art, artifacts, and historical objects reflecting the cultural heritage of Todi and the surrounding region.

Attractions:

1. Art Collections:

- Explore the museum's diverse art collections, featuring paintings, sculptures, and decorative arts from the Middle Ages to the modern era.

- Highlights include works by renowned Italian artists such as Niccolò di Liberatore, known as "L'Alunno," and Andrea della Robbia.

2. Historical Exhibits:

- Discover exhibits showcasing the history and culture of Todi, including archaeological finds, ancient artifacts, and medieval manuscripts.

- Learn about the city's development, architectural heritage, and notable figures through interactive displays and multimedia presentations.

Things to Do:

- Take a guided tour of Museo di Palazzo Buonaccorsi to gain insights into Todi's artistic and cultural heritage.

- Attend temporary exhibitions and special events held at the museum, featuring contemporary art, photography, and cultural performances.

- Explore the palace's elegant interiors, including its grand halls, frescoed ceilings, and ornate furnishings.

Visiting Museo di Palazzo Buonaccorsi offers a unique opportunity to immerse oneself in the history, art, and culture of Todi and gain a deeper appreciation for the city's rich heritage.

Foligno – Pinacoteca Civica (Civic Gallery)

Location: Corso Cavour, 88, 06034 Foligno PG, Italy

Phone Number: +39 0742 342302

Website: http://www.pinacotecafoligno.it/

Opening Hours:

- Tuesday to Sunday: 9:00 AM to 1:00 PM, 3:00 PM to 7:00 PM

- Closed on Mondays

Entry Fee:

- Regular: €5

- Reduced (students and seniors): €3

- Free for children below 18 and disabled visitors

History:

- Pinacoteca Civica, or the Civic Gallery, is housed in a historic building in the heart of Foligno's historic center.

- The gallery was founded in the late 19th century and houses a rich collection of paintings, sculptures, and decorative arts spanning the medieval to modern periods.

- Pinacoteca Civica is dedicated to preserving and showcasing the artistic heritage of Foligno and the surrounding region.

Attractions:

1. Art Collections:

- Explore the gallery's extensive art collections, featuring works by prominent Italian artists such as Perugino, Benozzo Gozzoli, and Gentile da Fabriano.

- Discover masterpieces of Renaissance, Baroque, and Neoclassical art, including religious paintings, portraits, and landscapes.

2. Temporary Exhibitions:

- Attend temporary exhibitions held at Pinacoteca Civica, featuring contemporary art, photography, and multimedia installations.

- Experience a dynamic range of artistic expressions and engage with innovative and thought-provoking works by local and international artists.

Things to Do:

- Take a guided tour of Pinacoteca Civica to learn about the history, significance, and artistic significance of the gallery's collections.

- Attend lectures, workshops, and cultural events organized by the gallery, providing opportunities for further exploration and dialogue about art and culture.

- Explore Foligno's historic center, including its charming streets, piazzas, and landmarks, before or after visiting Pinacoteca Civica.

Visiting Pinacoteca Civica offers a rich cultural experience, allowing visitors to immerse themselves in the art and history of Foligno and discover the diverse and vibrant artistic traditions of the region.

Cascata delle Marmore (Marmore Falls)

Location: Loc. Cascata delle Marmore, 05100 Terni TR, Italy

Phone Number: +39 0744 62436

Website: http://www.marmorefalls.it/

Opening Hours:

- From April to September: 9:00 AM to 7:00 PM

- From October to March: 9:00 AM to 5:00 PM

Entry Fee:

- Regular: €12

- Reduced (children 6-12 years old): €8

- Free for children under 6 years old

History:

- Cascata delle Marmore is a man-made waterfall created by the ancient Romans in the 3rd century BC.

- The waterfall was originally designed as a drainage system to divert water from the Velino River into the Nera River, preventing flooding in the surrounding plains.

- Over time, the waterfall became a scenic attraction and a symbol of natural beauty in the Umbria region.

Attractions:

1. Scenic Overlooks:

- Enjoy breathtaking panoramic views of Cascata delle Marmore from various scenic overlooks situated at different levels.

- Capture the beauty of the cascading water surrounded by lush greenery and rocky landscapes.

2. Walking Trails:

- Explore the well-maintained walking trails around the falls, providing opportunities for leisurely strolls and nature walks.

- Discover viewpoints along the trails, offering different perspectives of the waterfall.

3. Boat Tours:

- Take a boat tour on the lake at the base of the falls to experience the sheer power and beauty of Cascata delle Marmore up close.

- Boat tours provide a unique and refreshing way to appreciate the natural surroundings.

Things to Do:

- Participate in guided tours to learn about the history, geology, and ecological significance of Cascata delle Marmore.

- Enjoy outdoor activities such as hiking, picnicking, and bird watching in the surrounding natural reserve.

- Visit nearby attractions, including the ancient Roman ruins and historical sites in the Terni area.

A visit to Cascata delle Marmore offers a harmonious blend of natural beauty, history, and outdoor activities, providing a memorable experience for nature enthusiasts and adventure seekers alike.

Lake Trasimeno

Location: Umbria, Italy

As a natural lake, Lake Trasimeno does not have a specific phone number or entry fee. Below is information on general activities and attractions around the lake.

Website: https://www.lagotrasimeno.co.uk/

History:

- Lake Trasimeno, the largest lake in central Italy, has a rich history dating back to ancient times.

- The lake is renowned for the Battle of Lake Trasimeno in 217 BC, where Hannibal defeated the Roman army during the Second Punic War.

- Surrounded by picturesque landscapes and charming towns, Lake Trasimeno has been a source of inspiration for poets, artists, and nature lovers throughout the centuries.

Attractions:

1. Isola Maggiore:

  - Explore Isola Maggiore, the second-largest island on the lake, known for its tranquility and historic fishing traditions.

  - Visit the medieval village, enjoy scenic walks, and discover the island's cultural and natural heritage.

2. Isola Polvese:

- Experience the beauty of Isola Polvese, the largest island, characterized by lush vegetation, walking trails, and historical ruins.

- Visit the Botanical Garden and the Olive Oil Museum to learn about the island's flora and traditional olive oil production.

3. Towns around the Lake:

- Discover charming towns and villages around Lake Trasimeno, such as Castiglione del Lago, Passignano sul Trasimeno, and Tuoro sul Trasimeno.

- Enjoy lakeside promenades, historical architecture, and local cuisine in these picturesque locations.

Things to Do:

Boat Tours:

- Take a boat tour on Lake Trasimeno to enjoy scenic views and visit the islands.

- Boat tours often include stops at Isola Maggiore, Isola Polvese, and other points of interest.

Water Activities:

- Engage in water activities such as swimming, kayaking, and paddle boarding.

- Lake Trasimeno provides a refreshing and serene environment for water recreation.

Cycling and Hiking:

- Explore cycling and hiking trails around the lake, offering stunning vistas of the water and surrounding landscapes.

- Enjoy the natural beauty and tranquility of the lake's shores.

Local Cuisine:

- Indulge in the delicious local cuisine featuring fresh fish from the lake, regional wines, and traditional Umbrian dishes.

- Lakeside restaurants and cafes provide an idyllic setting for culinary experiences.

A visit to Lake Trasimeno offers a perfect blend of natural beauty, cultural exploration, and outdoor activities, providing a serene and enjoyable experience for visitors.

Montefalco – Sagrantino Vineyards

Location: Montefalco, Umbria, Italy

As vineyards are private properties, they may not have a specific phone number or entry fee. Below is general information on visiting Sagrantino Vineyards in Montefalco.

Website: (Sagrantino Vineyards may not have a dedicated website, but you can find information through local wineries or tourism websites.)

History:

- Montefalco is renowned for its production of Sagrantino wine, a unique and prestigious variety grown exclusively in the region.

- The history of Sagrantino wine dates back centuries, with references to its cultivation and consumption found in medieval texts and documents.

- Sagrantino grapes thrive in the fertile soil and favorable climate of Montefalco, producing rich and full-bodied wines prized by wine enthusiasts worldwide.

Attractions:

1. Vineyard Tours:

   - Experience guided tours of Sagrantino vineyards in Montefalco, offering insights into the winemaking process and the cultivation of Sagrantino grapes.

- Learn about the history and traditions of winemaking in the region from knowledgeable guides and winemakers.

2. Wine Tasting:

- Enjoy wine tastings at local wineries and cellars, sampling a variety of Sagrantino wines and other regional specialties.

- Learn about different vintages, flavors, and characteristics of Sagrantino wine through guided tasting sessions.

3. Scenic Views:

- Explore the picturesque landscapes surrounding Montefalco's vineyards, offering stunning views of rolling hills, olive groves, and medieval villages.

- Capture the beauty of the Umbrian countryside and vine-covered slopes during leisurely walks or bicycle rides.

Things to Do:

Visit Local Wineries:

- Explore family-owned wineries and larger estates in Montefalco, discovering the unique terroir and winemaking techniques of Sagrantino wine producers.

- Participate in cellar tours, barrel tastings, and educational workshops offered by wineries.

Cultural Exploration:

- Immerse yourself in the rich cultural heritage of Montefalco, known as the "Balcony of Umbria" for its panoramic views and historic landmarks.

- Visit Montefalco's medieval center, featuring charming streets, ancient churches, and Renaissance palaces.

Culinary Experiences:

- Pair your wine tasting experience with authentic Umbrian cuisine, featuring local delicacies such as truffles, olive oil, and pecorino cheese.

- Enjoy meals at traditional trattorias and restaurants, where you can savor the flavors of Umbrian's culinary traditions

A visit to Sagrantino Vineyards in Montefalco offers a memorable journey through the art, history, and flavors of one of Italy's most renowned wine regions.

Chapter 5

Accommodations

When it comes to finding the perfect place to stay in Umbria, you'll discover a diverse range of accommodations catering to different preferences and budgets. Whether you're seeking the charm of historic hotels, the tranquility of countryside retreats, or the convenience of modern resorts, Umbria has something to offer for every traveler.

Umbria offers a diverse array of accommodations to suit every traveler's preferences. From historic charm to modern luxury, the region provides a range of options for a memorable stay.

Here are the main types of accommodation in Umbria:

Historic Hotels:

1. Hotel Brufani Palace - Perugia

Description: Hotel Brufani Palace is a luxurious historic hotel located in the heart of Perugia. Dating back to the 19th century, it offers elegant accommodations, gourmet dining, and panoramic views of the surrounding countryside.

Address: Piazza Italia, 12, 06121 Perugia PG, Italy

Website: https://www.brufanipalace.com/

Opening Hours: Open 24 hours

Phone Number: +39 075 5732541

Price Range: €200 - €500 per night

2. Castello di Monterone - Perugia

Description: Castello di Monterone is a charming castle hotel situated just outside Perugia. Surrounded by olive groves and vineyards, it offers a peaceful retreat with medieval charm and modern amenities.

Address: Località Monterone, 06132 Perugia PG, Italy

Website: https://www.castellomonterone.com/

Opening Hours: Open 24 hours

Phone Number: +39 075 572 2679

Price Range: €150 - €400 per night

3. Palazzo Bontadosi Hotel & Spa - Montefalco

Description: Palazzo Bontadosi Hotel & Spa is housed in a beautifully restored 15th-century palace in the historic town of Montefalco. With its Renaissance architecture and modern comforts, it offers a blend of luxury and heritage.

Address: Piazza del Comune, 19, 06036 Montefalco PG, Italy

Website: https://www.palazzobontadosi.com/

Opening Hours: Open 24 hours

Phone Number: +39 0742 378490

Price Range: €180 - €450 per night

4. Hotel Le Tre Vaselle - Torgiano

Description: Hotel Le Tre Vaselle is a historic hotel nestled in the medieval village of Torgiano. Set within a former 17th-century villa, it offers refined accommodations, gourmet cuisine, and a renowned wine cellar.

Address: Via Garibaldi, 48, 06089 Torgiano PG, Italy

Website: [Hotel Le Tre Vaselle](https://www.3vaselle.it/)

Opening Hours: Open 24 hours

Phone Number: +39 075 9880447

Price Range: €160 - €400 per night

These historic hotels in Umbria offer travelers a unique blend of heritage, luxury, and comfort, ensuring a memorable stay in this enchanting region.

Modern Resorts

While Umbria is renowned for its historic charm, it also offers modern resorts that seamlessly blend contemporary luxury with the region's natural beauty. Here are four modern resorts in Umbria, each with its unique features:

1. Palazzo Seneca - Norcia

Description: Palazzo Seneca is a luxurious modern resort located in the heart of Norcia. This boutique hotel combines sleek, modern design with a tranquil setting. Guests can enjoy well-appointed rooms, a spa, and gourmet dining.

Address: Via Cesare Battisti, 12, 06046 Norcia PG, Italy

Website: https://www.palazzoseneca.com/

Opening Hours: Open 24 hours

Phone Number: +39 0743 817434

Price Range: €200 - €600 per night

2. Villa Roncalli - Foligno

Description: Villa Roncalli is a modern resort set in a historic villa just outside Foligno. With contemporary design and lush gardens, the resort provides a peaceful retreat. Amenities include a swimming pool, wellness center, and stylish accommodations.

Address: Strada dei Conti, 1, 06034 Foligno PG, Italy

Website: https://www.villaroncalli.it/

Opening Hours: Open 24 hours

Phone Number: +39 0742 340341

Price Range: €150 - €400 per night

3. Residenza Fontanelle - Perugia

Description: Residenza Fontanelle is a modern resort perched on the hills overlooking Perugia. The resort offers contemporary suites with panoramic views, an outdoor pool, and a wellness center. It's an ideal blend of modern luxury and natural serenity.

Address: Via Beato Placido Riccardi, 2, 06134 Perugia PG, Italy

Website: https://www.residenzafontanelle.com/

Opening Hours: Open 24 hours

Phone Number: +39 075 572 4125

Price Range: €180 - €500 per night

4. Antico Borgo di Tabiano Castello - Gubbio

Description: This modern resort is set in an ancient castle near Gubbio. With its contemporary interiors and medieval backdrop, Antico Borgo di Tabiano Castello offers a unique experience. Guests can enjoy spacious rooms, a pool, and panoramic terraces.

Address: Località Tabiano, 06024 Gubbio PG, Italy

Website: https://www.anticoborgoditabiano.it/

Opening Hours: Open 24 hours

Phone Number: +39 075 927 9290

Price Range: €120 - €350 per night

These modern resorts in Umbria cater to those seeking contemporary comforts amid the region's timeless landscapes.

Bed and Breakfasts (B&Bs)

Here are four charming Bed and Breakfasts (B&Bs) for you in Umbria along with their details:

1. Il Roseto Bed and Breakfast - Perugia

Description: Il Roseto Bed and Breakfast is a cozy retreat located in Perugia. Set in a historic building, it offers personalized hospitality, comfortable rooms, and a delightful garden for guests to enjoy.

Address: Via Solitaria, 4, 06122 Perugia PG, Italy

Website: http://www.ilrosuetoperugia.it/

Opening Hours: Open 24 hours

Phone Number: +39 075 5721764

Price Range: €70 - €150 per night

2. La Terrazza del Subasio Bed and Breakfast - Assisi

Description: La Terrazza del Subasio Bed and Breakfast is situated in the heart of Assisi. With a welcoming atmosphere, panoramic views, and comfortable accommodations, it provides an ideal base for exploring the historic town.

Address: Via S. Francesco, 18, 06081 Assisi PG, Italy

Website: http://www.laterrazzadelsubasio.it/

Opening Hours: Open 24 hours

Phone Number: +39 075 812264

Price Range: €80 - €130 per night

3. B&B Alla Mariuca - Spoleto

Description: B&B Alla Mariuca is a charming accommodation in Spoleto, known for its warm hospitality and homely ambiance. Guests can enjoy a comfortable stay in this family-run B&B surrounded by the scenic Umbrian hills.

Address: Via Fratelli Bandiera, 9, 06049 Spoleto PG, Italy

Website: http://www.allamariuca.it/

Opening Hours: Open 24 hours

Phone Number: +39 0743 49577

Price Range: €60 - €120 per night

4. La Collina Bed and Breakfast - Todi

Description: La Collina Bed and Breakfast is perched on a hill near Todi, offering breathtaking views of the Umbrian countryside. With its rustic charm, comfortable rooms, and a friendly atmosphere, it provides a tranquil escape.

Address: Località Cordigliano, 43, 06059 Todi PG, Italy

Website: http://www.lacollinabedandbreakfast.it/

Opening Hours: Open 24 hours

Phone Number: +39 075 8948322

Price Range: €80 - €150 per night

These Bed and Breakfasts in Umbria offer a personal touch, allowing guests to experience the warmth of local hospitality in picturesque surroundings.

Agriturismi (Farm Stays)

For a rural escape, agriturismi provide an authentic experience in the Umbrian countryside. Set amidst vineyards and olive groves, these farm stays allow guests to immerse themselves in traditional farming practices and enjoy the beauty of nature.

1. Agriturismo Il Sarale - Assisi

Description: Agriturismo Il Sarale is a delightful farm stay located near Assisi. Surrounded by olive groves and vineyards, this agriturismo offers guests a genuine rural experience with comfortable

accommodations and traditional Umbrian cuisine.
Address: Via Campiglione, 7, 06081 Assisi PG, Italy.

Website: https://www.ilsarale.it/

Opening Hours: Open 24 hours

Phone Number: +39 075 816601

Price Range: €80 - €150 per night

2. Agriturismo La volpe e l'uva - Perugia

Description: Agriturismo La volpe e l'uva is a charming farm stay nestled in the hills near Perugia. With its vineyards, orchards, and comfortable rooms, guests can experience the tranquility of the Umbrian countryside.

Address: Via Colle Marzio, 7, 06132 Perugia PG, Italy

Website: https://www.lavolpeeluva.it/

Opening Hours: Open 24 hours

Phone Number: +39 075 603131

Price Range: €70 - €130 per night

3. Agriturismo Il Melograno - Todi

Description: Agriturismo Il Melograno is a serene farm stay located near Todi. Set within an organic farm, guests can enjoy the beauty of nature, participate in farm activities, and savor delicious organic produce.

Address: Località Pian di Pieca, 33, 06059 Todi PG, Italy

Website: https://www.agriturismoilmelograno.eu/

Opening Hours: Open 24 hours

Phone Number: +39 340 6140730

Price Range: €80 - €120 per night

4. Agriturismo La Locanda del Prete - Montefalco

Description: Agriturismo La Locanda del Prete is a rustic farm stay nestled in the Montefalco countryside. With its vineyards, olive groves, and traditional stone farmhouse, it offers a tranquil retreat with authentic Umbrian hospitality.

Address: Località Cerrete, 06036 Montefalco PG, Italy

Website: https://www.lalocandadelprete.it/

Opening Hours: Open 24 hours

Phone Number: +39 0742 379189

Price Range: €90 - €160 per night

These Agriturismi (Farm Stays) in Umbria provide guests with an immersive experience in the region's agricultural traditions, offering a perfect blend of nature, comfort, and authentic local cuisine.

Boutique Inns

Boutique inns in Umbria are characterized by their unique design, smaller size, and curated ambiance. These establishments often showcase regional artwork and design elements, offering a more personalized and stylish stay.

1. Relais La Corte di Bettona - Bettona

Description: Relais La Corte di Bettona is a charming boutique inn located in the medieval town of Bettona. Set within a historic building, it offers elegant rooms, a rooftop terrace with panoramic views, and a delightful courtyard.

Address: Via Santa Caterina, 2, 06084 Bettona PG, Italy

Website: https://www.lacortedibettona.it/

Opening Hours: Open 24 hours

Phone Number: +39 075 9880370

Price Range: €120 - €300 per night

2. Borgo dei Conti Resort - Perugia

Description: Borgo dei Conti Resort is a luxurious boutique inn set within a historic estate near Perugia. With its refined accommodations, spa facilities, and beautifully landscaped gardens, it offers a serene escape in a sophisticated setting.

Address: Località Borgo dei Conti, 19, 06074 Collepepe PG, Italy

Website: https://www.borgodeicontiresort.it/

Opening Hours: Open 24 hours

Phone Number: +39 075 8716950

Price Range: €200 - €600 per night

3. Palazzo Bontadosi Hotel & Spa - Montefalco

Description: Palazzo Bontadosi Hotel & Spa is a boutique inn situated in the historic town of Montefalco. Housed within a beautifully restored 15th-century palace, it offers a blend of historic charm, modern comforts, and spa facilities.

Address: Piazza del Comune, 19, 06036 Montefalco PG, Italy

Website: https://www.palazzobontadosi.com/

Opening Hours: Open 24 hours

Phone Number: +39 0742 378490

Price Range: €180 - €450 per night

4. Hotel Giotto Assisi - Assisi

Description: Hotel Giotto Assisi is a boutique inn located in the heart of Assisi. With its central location, stylish decor, and personalized service, it provides guests with a comfortable and chic retreat in this historic town.

Address: Via Fontebella, 41, 06081 Assisi PG, Italy

Website: https://www.hotelgiottoassisi.it/

Opening Hours: Open 24 hours

Phone Number: +39 075 812405

Price Range: €100 - €250 per night

These Boutique Inns in Umbria offer travelers a unique and stylish retreat, combining personalized service with a sophisticated ambiance for a memorable stay in the region.

Holiday Apartments/Villas

1. Villa Panorama - Perugia

Description: Villa Panorama is a spacious holiday villa with panoramic views, located near Perugia. This self-catering accommodation features a private pool, modern amenities, and ample outdoor space for a relaxing stay.

Address: Via dei Fontanili, 06134 Perugia PG, Italy

Website: https://www.villapanoramaumbria.it/

Opening Hours: Open 24 hours

Phone Number: +39 347 7471717

Price Range: €150 - €350 per night

2. Casa del Borgo - Assisi

Description: Casa del Borgo is a charming holiday apartment situated in the historic center of Assisi. With its rustic decor and central location, it provides a cozy retreat for guests exploring the town's cultural and culinary delights.

Address: Vicolo S. Andrea, 3, 06081 Assisi PG, Italy

Website: https://www.casadelborgoassisi.com/

Opening Hours: Open 24 hours

Phone Number: +39 075 813714

Price Range: €80 - €200 per night

3. Umbria Loft - Todi

Description: Umbria Loft is a stylish holiday apartment located in the heart of Todi.

With its modern design, fully equipped kitchen, and proximity to local attractions, it offers a comfortable and convenient stay.

Address: Via della Maleretta, 7, 06059 Todi PG, Italy

Website: https://www.umbrialoft.com/

Opening Hours: Open 24 hours

Phone Number: +39 331 407 7633

Price Range: €90 - €180 per night

4. Agriturismo Il Bastione – Montefalco

Description: Agriturismo Il Bastione offers holiday apartments within a farmhouse setting near Montefalco. Guests can enjoy the tranquility of the Umbrian countryside, a shared pool, and comfortable accommodations with rustic charm.

Address: Strada Comunale di Montecchio, 06036 Montefalco PG, Italy

Website: http://www.agriturismoilbastione.it/

Opening Hours: Open 24 hours

Phone Number: +39 339 344 0213

Price Range: €80 - €150 per night

These holiday apartments and villas in Umbria offer guests the flexibility and comfort of a home away from home, providing an ideal base for exploring the region's beauty and attractions.

Guesthouses

Guesthouses in Umbria offer a comfortable and affordable stay. They vary in size and style, providing a welcoming atmosphere for travelers seeking a more laid-back experience.

Finding budget-friendly guesthouses in Umbria can add to the charm of your stay.

1. Le Terre di Isa - Assisi

Description: Le Terre di Isa is a budget-friendly guesthouse located near Assisi. Offering simple yet comfortable rooms, it provides a peaceful retreat amidst the Umbrian countryside.

Address: Via Francesco Pizzoni, 7, 06081 Assisi PG, Italy

Website: https://www.leterrediisa.com/

Opening Hours: Open 24 hours

Phone Number: +39 075 813130

Price Range: €50 - €100 per night

2. Ostello Victor Center - Perugia

Description: Ostello Victor Center is a budget-friendly hostel in Perugia. With shared dormitories and basic amenities, it provides an affordable option for budget-conscious travelers.

Address: Via Eugubina, 42, 06121 Perugia PG, Italy

Website: https://www.ostellovictorcenter.com/

Opening Hours: Open 24 hours

Phone Number: +39 075 572 0118

Price Range: €20 - €50 per night (dormitory options available)

3. Green House Assisi - Assisi

Description: Green House Assisi is a budget guesthouse located in Assisi. With simple accommodations and a welcoming atmosphere, it offers an affordable option for travelers exploring the town.

Address: Via Frate Elia, 3, 06081 Assisi PG, Italy

Website: http://www.greenhouseassisi.com/

Opening Hours: Open 24 hours

Phone Number: +39 075 802 3815

Price Range: €40 - €80 per night

4. Hostel Perugia Centro - Perugia

Description: Hostel Perugia Centro is a budget hostel located in the center of Perugia. With shared dormitories and budget-friendly prices, it caters to travelers looking for economical accommodation.

Address: Via Campo Battaglia, 22, 06122 Perugia PG, Italy

Website: https://www.perugiacentro.it/

Opening Hours: Open 24 hours

Phone Number: +39 075 572 3786

Price Range: €20 - €50 per night (dormitory options available

These budget guesthouses in Umbria offer affordable accommodations without compromising on comfort, making them suitable options for travelers on a budget.

Hostels

Budget-conscious travelers can find hostels in urban centers or popular tourist destinations in Umbria. These provide shared accommodations and facilities for those looking for affordable stays.

Finding economical hostels in Umbria can be a great option for budget-conscious travelers. Here are two budget-friendly hostels in the region:

1. Ostello Victor Center - Perugia

Description: Ostello Victor Center is a budget-friendly hostel located in Perugia. It offers shared dormitories with basic amenities, making it an affordable choice for travelers on a budget.

Address: Via Eugubina, 42, 06121 Perugia PG, Italy

Website: https://www.ostellovictorcenter.com/

Opening Hours: Open 24 hours

Phone Number: +39 075 572 0118

Price Range: €20 - €50 per night (dormitory options available)

2. Hostel Perugia Centro - Perugia

Description: Hostel Perugia Centro is a budget hostel situated in the heart of Perugia. It offers shared dormitories and budget-friendly prices, providing a convenient and economical accommodation option.

Address: Via Campo Battaglia, 22, 06122 Perugia PG, Italy

Website: https://www.perugiacentro.it/

Opening Hours: Open 24 hours

Phone Number: +39 075 572 3786

Price Range: €20 - €50 per night (dormitory options available)

These hostels in Umbria cater to travelers seeking budget-friendly accommodation options, providing a social atmosphere and basic amenities for a comfortable stay.

Choosing the right type of accommodation in Umbria allows you to tailor their experience, ensuring a comfortable and memorable stay in this enchanting region. Whether you choose a historic hotel in the heart of Perugia, a charming B&B overlooking Lake Trasimeno or an agriturismo in the rolling hills, your choice of accommodation will play a pivotal role in shaping your Umbrian experience.

Chapter 6

Culinary Delights in Umbria

Umbria, the heart of Italy, is not only renowned for its captivating landscapes and rich history but also for its exceptional culinary offerings that reflect the region's cultural heritage and dedication to gastronomic excellence.

This chapter explores the delectable world of Umbrian cuisine, inviting you to embark on a gastronomic journey that unveils the flavors, traditions, and stories behind the region's culinary delights.

Umbrian's culinary identity is deeply rooted in the region's fertile lands, where olive groves, vineyards, and truffle-rich forests shape the ingredients that define its dishes. From the ancient hilltop towns to the bustling markets, Umbrian's food culture is a testament to the symbiotic relationship between the land and its people.

Traditional Umbrian Cuisines

1. Pasta alla Norcina:

Description: Pasta alla Norcina is a rich pasta dish originating from Norcia, Umbria, featuring fresh pasta tossed in a creamy sauce made with pork sausage, cream, and black truffles.

Nutritional Description: This dish is high in protein from the pork sausage and provides energy from the carbohydrates in the pasta. The cream adds richness and flavor, while the truffles impart a unique earthy taste.

Taste: Pasta alla Norcina is indulgent and savory, with the richness of the cream complementing the earthiness of the truffles and the savory flavors of the sausage.

2. Strangozzi al Tartufo:

Description: Strangozzi al Tartufo is a traditional Umbrian pasta dish made with long, thick strands of pasta served with a sauce made from butter, garlic, and shaved black truffles.

Nutritional Description: This dish provides carbohydrates from the pasta and healthy fats from the butter.

The truffles add a distinctive flavor and aroma while contributing antioxidants and other beneficial compounds.

Taste: Strangozzi al Tartufo is rich and aromatic, with the buttery sauce enhancing the earthy flavors of the truffles. The dish has a luxurious texture and a satisfying taste.

3. Porchetta:

Description: Porchetta is a traditional Italian pork roast, popular in Umbria, where the whole pig is deboned, seasoned with herbs such as rosemary, garlic, and fennel, and then slow-roasted until tender.

Nutritional Description: Porchetta is rich in protein and provides essential nutrients such as iron and B vitamins. It is relatively high in fat but also offers a good amount of selenium, an antioxidant mineral.

Taste: Porchetta is succulent and flavorful, with the aromatic herbs infusing the meat with savory notes. The crispy skin adds texture, while the tender, juicy meat melts in the mouth, making it a favorite among locals and visitors alike.

4. Torta al Testo:

Description: Torta al Testo is a traditional Umbrian flatbread made from simple dough of flour, water, yeast, and olive oil, cooked on a terracotta griddle called a "testo."

Nutritional Description: This flatbread is low in fat and provides carbohydrates for energy. It is also a good source of dietary fiber and contains some protein from the flour.

Taste: Torta al Testo has a rustic, slightly chewy texture with a subtle olive oil flavor. It pairs well with a variety of toppings, such as cured meats, cheese, and vegetables, making it a versatile and satisfying staple of Umbrian cuisine.

5. Lenticchie di Castelluccio:

Description: Lenticchie di Castelluccio refers to lentils cultivated in the plains of Castelluccio di Norcia. These small, flavorful lentils are often used in hearty soups, stews, or as a side dish.

Nutritional Description: Lentils are an excellent source of plant-based protein, fiber, and essential minerals such as iron and folate. They are low in fat and provide a sustained release of energy.

Taste: Lenticchie di Castelluccio has a robust, earthy flavor and a firm texture. When cooked, they absorb the flavors of the surrounding ingredients, making them a versatile and nutritious addition to various dishes.

6. Pappa al Pomodoro:

Description: Pappa al Pomodoro is a traditional Tuscan dish that has found its way into Umbrian cuisine. It is a thick soup made with stale bread, tomatoes, garlic, basil, and olive oil.

Nutritional Description: This dish offers carbohydrates from the bread, antioxidants from tomatoes, and heart-healthy monounsaturated fats from olive oil. It is relatively low in calories and provides a comforting, filling meal.

Taste: Pappa al Pomodoro has a comforting and hearty taste. The combination of tomatoes, garlic, and basil creates a savory and aromatic flavor profile, while the bread adds a satisfying texture.

7. Tagliata di Chianina:

Description: Tagliata di Chianina is a dish featuring sliced beef from the renowned Chianina cattle breed, typically cooked rare to medium-rare and seasoned with olive oil, salt, and rosemary.

Nutritional Description: Chianina beef is lean and provides high-quality protein, iron, and zinc. Olive oil contributes heart-healthy fats, and rosemary adds antioxidants and flavor.

Taste: Tagliata di Chianina offers a robust beefy flavor with a hint of rosemary. The meat is tender and juicy, making it a favorite for meat lovers seeking a taste of Umbrian excellence.

8. Tartufo Nero Gelato:

Description: Umbria is famous for its truffles, and Tartufo Nero Gelato is a delightful dessert featuring black truffle-flavored gelato, capturing the essence of the region's prized delicacy.

Nutritional Description: Gelato is lower in fat than traditional ice cream and offers a sweet treat with the distinct earthy taste of truffles.

Taste: Tartufo Nero Gelato provides a unique combination of sweet and savory flavors. The earthiness of the truffles in the gelato creates a memorable and unexpected dessert experience.

Dining Etiquette

Understanding dining etiquette is essential when experiencing Umbrian cuisine. Here are some key points you observe:

1. Respect for Meal Times:

In Umbria, meals are viewed as a time for gathering, socializing, and enjoying food. Lunch is typically the main meal of the day and is often enjoyed leisurely, with family and friends. Dinner is also an important affair, but tends to be lighter and eaten later in the evening.

2. Greeting and Seating:

Upon entering a restaurant or home, it is customary to greet the host or restaurant staff warmly.

Seating arrangements are usually organized by the host or staff, with guests seated according to age or status.

3. Bread and Olive Oil:

Bread and olive oil are common staples on the table. It is polite to wait until everyone is seated before breaking bread and dipping it in olive oil. Bread should never be placed upside down on the table, as it is considered disrespectful.

4. Ordering and Service:

In restaurants, it is customary to wait for the server to take your order rather than signaling or calling them over. Once you have placed your order, be patient and enjoy the leisurely pace of dining in Umbria. It isn't uncommon for meals to be served in multiple courses.

5. Use of Utensils:

Use utensils appropriately, starting from the outside and working your way in with each course. Keep your hands visible above the table at all times and refrain from resting your elbows on the table, which is considered impolite.

6. Engagement in Conversation:

Engage in conversation with your dining companions, but avoid discussing sensitive topics such as politics or religion. Instead, focus on enjoying the meal and sharing pleasant anecdotes or experiences.

7. Wine and Toasting:

Wine is an integral part of Umbrian dining culture. It is customary for the host or server to pour wine for guests, so avoid refilling your glass yourself. When making a toast, maintain eye contact and clink glasses gently.

8. Expressing Gratitude:

At the end of the meal, it is customary to express gratitude to the host or restaurant staff for their hospitality. A simple "Grazie" (thank you) or "Grazie mille" (thank you very much) is appropriate.

Observing these dining etiquettes not only shows respect for Umbrian culture but also enhances your dining experience, allowing you to fully appreciate the flavors and traditions of the region.

Umbrian Wines and Wineries

Umbria, often overshadowed by its neighboring wine powerhouse, Tuscany, is a hidden gem for wine enthusiasts. The region is home to unique grape varieties and boasts wineries that produce exceptional wines. Here's a glimpse into Umbrian wines and some notable wineries:

1. Sagrantino:

Description: Sagrantino is the flagship red wine of Umbria, primarily produced around the town of Montefalco. Known for its robust character, deep color, and high tannins, Sagrantino wines age well and often exhibit complex flavors of dark fruit, spices, and tobacco.

Notable Wineries: Arnaldo Caprai, Tabarrini, Paolo Bea

2. Montefalco Rosso:

Description: Montefalco Rosso is a red blend that typically includes Sangiovese, Sagrantino, and other local grape varieties. These wines are approachable at a younger age than pure Sagrantino and offer a harmonious combination of fruitiness and structure.

Notable Wineries: Lungarotti, Perticaia, Antonelli San Marco

3. Orvieto Classico:

Description: Orvieto Classico is a well-known white wine produced in the Orvieto region. Typically a blend of Trebbiano and Grechetto grapes, these wines are crisp, refreshing, and often display floral and citrus notes.

Notable Wineries: Palazzone, Decugnano dei Barbi, Barberani

4. Grechetto:

Description: Grechetto is a white grape variety indigenous to Umbria. Wines made from Grechetto are aromatic, with flavors ranging from floral and fruity to herbal. They often have a good balance of acidity, making them versatile for various occasions.

Notable Wineries: Lungarotti, Roccafiore, Castello delle Regine

5. Sangiovese:

Description: While Sangiovese is more commonly associated with Tuscany, it is also grown in Umbria. Umbrian Sangiovese wines are medium-bodied, with bright acidity and flavors of red fruit, making them approachable and food-friendly.

Notable Wineries: Scacciadiavoli, Falesco, Tenuta Bellafonte

6. Umbria Bianco:

Description: Umbria Bianco wines are white blends that may include Trebbiano, Grechetto, and other local grape varieties. These wines are often refreshing, with a mix of citrus, floral, and herbal notes.

Notable Wineries: Lungarotti, Castello delle Regine, Caprai

7. Winery Experiences:

Arnaldo Caprai: Known for its pioneering work with Sagrantino, Arnaldo Caprai offers guided tours and tastings, providing insights into the winemaking process.

Lungarotti: A historic winery with a commitment to sustainability, Lungarotti offers tours of its vineyards, cellars, and olive oil production, accompanied by tastings.

Tabarrini: Tabarrini focuses on organic farming and produces outstanding Sagrantino wines. Their winery tours offer a glimpse into their biodynamic practices.

Exploring the wineries and wines of Umbria is a journey into the region's rich viticultural heritage, where tradition meets innovation, resulting in a diverse and compelling wine scene.

Coffee Culture

In Umbria, as in much of Italy, coffee is not just a beverage; it's a way of life. The rich coffee culture is deeply ingrained in the daily routines and social fabric of the region. Here's a closer look at Umbrian's coffee culture:

1. Espresso Tradition:

Umbria, like the rest of Italy, embraces the art of espresso. Locals prefer short, strong shots of coffee that pack a punch. Ordering a simple "caffè" will get you a shot of espresso, the purest form of Italian coffee.

2. Cappuccino Rules:

 - Cappuccino is a breakfast delight in Umbria, but it comes with a set of unwritten rules. It's typically consumed only in the morning, and never after a meal. Italians believe that the combination of milk and coffee aids digestion, making it an ideal start to the day.

3. The Art of Lingering:

Unlike the hurried coffee culture in some places, enjoying coffee in Umbria is an unhurried affair. Locals savor their coffee slowly, often standing at the bar or sitting at a café table, engaging in leisurely conversation with friends or reading the newspaper.

4. Iconic Coffee Establishments:

Umbria is home to charming cafés and historic establishments where coffee is an experience, not just a beverage. From quaint local bars to elegant espresso lounges, each venue has its own unique ambiance, contributing to the rich tapestry of Umbrian coffee culture.

5. Espresso Varieties:

While a classic espresso is the go-to choice, you'll find variations like macchiato (espresso with a splash of milk), ristretto (an even shorter and more concentrated shot), and lungo (a longer shot with more water). Each variety caters to different preferences and occasions.

6. Coffee and Community:

Coffee in Umbria is not just about the drink; it's about community. The local bar or café is a gathering place where friends catch up, locals share stories, and visitors experience the warmth of Umbrian hospitality.

Culinary Adventures and Cooking Classes

1. Truffle Hunting Excursions:

To join truffle hunting excursions, you can book guided tours through local tour operators or truffle farms in Umbria. Many tour packages include transportation, truffle hunting demonstrations, tastings, and sometimes even cooking classes featuring truffle-infused dishes.

2. Farm-to-Table Experiences:

Farm-to-table experiences can be arranged through agriturismi (farm stays), where you can participate in farm activities, harvest produce, and join cooking sessions using fresh ingredients sourced directly from the farm.

3. Pasta Making Workshops:

Pasta making workshops are often offered by cooking schools, agriturismi, and culinary tour companies throughout Umbria. Look for classes advertised online, check with local visitor centers, or ask your accommodations for recommendations and assistance with booking.

4. Wine Tasting Tours:

Wine tasting tours can be arranged through local wineries or tour operators specializing in wine tourism. Some wineries offer scheduled tours and tastings, while others may require reservations in advance. Check winery websites, tour listings, or contact them directly to inquire about availability and booking procedures.

5. Cooking Classes with Local Chefs:

 - Cooking classes with local chefs can be arranged through cooking schools, restaurants, or accommodations that offer culinary experiences. Look for cooking class listings online, read reviews, and contact the organizers to inquire about class schedules, availability, and booking requirements.

6. Olive Oil Tasting Experiences:

Olive oil tasting experiences are often offered by olive oil producers, agriturismi, and specialty shops throughout Umbria. Look for listings of olive oil tasting events, workshops, or tours, and inquire about participation requirements and booking procedures.

7. Food Tours in Historic Towns:

Food tours in historic towns can be organized through local tour companies, culinary associations, or guided tour operators. Join scheduled tours or arrange private tours tailored to your preferences. Check tour listings, read reviews, and contact the organizers to book your culinary exploration of Umbrian's historic towns.

8. Cheese Making Workshops:

 - Cheese making workshops may be offered by cheese producers, agriturismi, or cooking schools specializing in cheese-centric culinary experiences. Research cheese making workshops online, inquire with local cheese producers, or ask your accommodations for recommendations and assistance with booking.

Chapter 7

Shopping in Umbria

Souvenirs and Local Crafts

1. Perugia - Artigianato Umbro

Location: Piazza IV Novembre, 06123 Perugia PG, Italy

Goods and Services: Artigianato Umbro specializes in handmade Umbrian souvenirs and crafts. Explore a wide range of items, including traditional ceramics, textiles, and trinkets. The boutique also offers personalized artisanal creations, allowing visitors to take home unique and customized mementos.

2. Assisi - La Bottega dell'Artigiano

Location: Via San Francesco, 25, 06081 Assisi PG, Italy Goods and Services: La Bottega dell'Artigiano is a charming boutique in Assisi, offering a diverse selection of locally crafted souvenirs.

From olive wood items to handmade jewelry, the shop focuses on showcasing the artistic talent of Assisi's craftsmen. Visitors can expect high-quality, handcrafted pieces that capture the spirit of the region.

3. Spello - Cose d'Altrove

Location: Via Giulia, 66, 06038 Spello PG, Italy

Goods and Services: Cose d'Altrove in Spello provides an eclectic collection of souvenirs and crafts. From hand-painted tiles to bespoke leather goods, the shop features a variety of locally made products. Visitors can explore unique offerings that reflect the diversity of Umbrian craftsmanship, ensuring a memorable shopping experience.

Markets and Bazaars

1. Perugia - Mercato Coperto

Location: Piazza Matteotti, 06121 Perugia PG, Italy

Goods and Services: Mercato Coperto in Perugia is a covered market offering a sensory experience for visitors. Explore stalls featuring fresh produce, artisanal products, and local delicacies.

Engage with vendors offering a range of goods, including Umbrian cheeses, cured meats, and handmade crafts. The market provides a dynamic atmosphere where visitors can immerse themselves in Umbrian's culinary delights.

2. Spoleto - Mercato delle Gaite

Location: Various locations in Spoleto

Goods and Services: Mercato delle Gaite in Spoleto is a unique historical market that recreates the atmosphere of medieval Umbria. Visitors can peruse stalls offering period-specific goods, from traditional clothing to artisanal crafts. Engage with costumed vendors and experience the rich history of Umbria through the diverse offerings of this annual market.

3. Gubbio - Mercato delle Erbe

Location: Piazza 40 Martiri, 06024 Gubbio PG, Italy

Goods and Services: Mercato delle Erbe in Gubbio is a local market showcasing the flavors of Umbria. Explore stalls featuring fresh produce, meats, and regional specialties.

Visitors can engage with local vendors, sample Umbrian products, and enjoy the lively atmosphere of this bustling market square.

Unique Shopping Districts

1. Perugia - Corso Vannucci

Location: Corso Vannucci, 06123 Perugia PG, Italy

Goods and Services: Corso Vannucci in Perugia is a bustling street lined with boutique shops, cafes, and cultural landmarks. Explore a vibrant mix of high-end fashion, artisanal crafts, and charming cafes. Visitors can shop for designer clothing, accessories, and handmade Umbrian products while taking in the historic architecture and lively atmosphere.

2. Assisi - Via San Francesco

Location: Via San Francesco, 06081 Assisi PG, Italy

Goods and Services: Via San Francesco in Assisi is a picturesque street adorned with boutiques and artisanal shops. Explore a blend of contemporary fashion, local crafts, and unique finds.

Visitors can shop for locally made clothing, accessories, and handmade goods, immersing themselves in the charming ambiance of this historic shopping district.

3. Todi - Via Roma

Location: Via Roma, Todi, Italy

Goods and Services: Via Roma in Todi is a central shopping hub, offering a mix of local boutiques and international brands. Explore a variety of shops offering clothing, accessories, and artisanal products. Visitors can shop for the latest fashion trends or discover unique Umbrian treasures while enjoying the charming streets and historic architecture.

4. Orvieto - Corso Cavour

Location: Corso Cavour, 05018 Orvieto TR, Italy

Goods and Services: Corso Cavour in Orvieto is a bustling avenue that combines modern elegance with historical charm. Explore a variety of shops offering fashion, accessories, and artisanal products.

Visitors can shop for unique clothing items, accessories, and Umbrian specialties while savoring the lively atmosphere and architectural beauty.

5. Foligno - Via Gramsci

Location: Via Gramsci, Foligno, Italy

Goods and Services: Via Gramsci in Foligno is a lively street known for its diverse shopping scene. Visitors can explore local boutiques and specialty stores offering clothing, accessories, and artisanal products. Whether seeking trendy fashion or traditional crafts, Via Gramsci provides a vibrant shopping experience in the heart of Foligno.

6. Città di Castello - Corso Cavour

Location: Corso Cavour, Città di Castello, Italy

Goods and Services: Corso Cavour in Città di Castello is a charming street offering a blend of traditional craftsmanship and modern trends. Visitors can explore local boutiques and specialty stores showcasing clothing, accessories, and artisanal products.

Enjoy the historic architecture and personalized shopping experience in this unique district.

7. Montefalco - Via Ringhiera Umbra

Location: Via Ringhiera Umbra, 06036 Montefalco PG, Italy

Goods and Services: Montefalco's Via Ringhiera Umbra is a picturesque street offering a mix of artisanal shops and boutiques. Visitors can discover locally crafted goods, including textiles, ceramics, and more. The scenic surroundings add to the appeal, creating a delightful destination for those seeking unique Umbrian treasures.

8. Spello - Via Giulia

Location: Via Giulia, 06038 Spello PG, Italy

Goods and Services: Via Giulia in Spello is a charming street lined with artisanal shops and boutiques. Visitors can explore the narrow alleys and discover hidden gems, from handmade jewelry to locally crafted goods. The intimate atmosphere and personalized service make Via Giulia a delightful spot for discerning shoppers.

9. Norcia - Via Umberto I

Location: Via Umberto I, 06046 Norcia PG, Italy

Goods and Services: Via Umberto I in Norcia is a bustling avenue known for its diverse shopping options. Visitors can explore shops offering local delicacies, handmade crafts, and Umbrian specialties. From gourmet treats to traditional crafts, Via Umberto I provides a vibrant shopping experience catering to various tastes and preferences.

Chapter 8

Festivals and Events - Celebrating Umbrian's Rich Heritage

Immerse yourself in the vibrant tapestry of Umbrian's cultural calendar as we explore the diverse festivals and events that grace this enchanting region throughout the year. From ancient traditions to contemporary celebrations, each event offers a unique opportunity to witness the essence of Umbrian's rich heritage.

Annual Celebrations

Umbria Jazz Festival, Perugia

Period: July

Location: Various venues in Perugia

Uniqueness: Renowned worldwide, the Umbria Jazz Festival transforms Perugia into a musical haven, featuring international jazz artists and vibrant performances across the city.

Festa dei Ceri, Gubbio

Period: May 15th

Location: Historic center of Gubbio

Uniqueness: Dating back to the Middle Ages, the Festa dei Ceri is a thrilling race where participants carry large wooden structures through narrow streets, honoring the patron saint Sant'Ubaldo. The event captivates spectators with its unique blend of athleticism and tradition.

Festival delle Nazioni, Città di Castello

Period: September

Location: Various venues in Città di Castello

Uniqueness: The Festival delle Nazioni celebrates cultural diversity through music, dance, and art, bringing together performers from around the world to showcase their talents in the picturesque town of Città di Castello.

Festival dei Due Mondi, Spoleto

Period: June-July

Location: Various venues in Spoleto

Uniqueness: A prestigious cultural event, the Festival dei Due Mondi showcases a fusion of music, theater, dance, and visual arts. International artists converge in Spoleto to present captivating productions against the backdrop of historic landmarks.

Calendimaggio, Assisi

Period: May

Location: Historic center of Assisi

Uniqueness: Transporting visitors to the Middle Ages, Calendimaggio is a vibrant celebration of spring featuring period costumes, music, and performances. The event creates a magical atmosphere in the historic streets of Assisi.

Cultural Events

Umbria Film Festival, Montone

Period: July

Location: Various cinemas in Montone

Uniqueness: Celebrating independent and international cinema, the Umbria Film Festival in Montone provides film enthusiasts with the opportunity to explore thought-provoking productions and engage with filmmakers.

Trasimeno Blues Festival, Lake Trasimeno

Period: July-August

Location: Various venues around Lake Trasimeno

Uniqueness: Set against the stunning backdrop of Lake Trasimeno, the Trasimeno Blues Festival features renowned blues artists from around the world, captivating audiences with soulful performances and lakeside concerts.

Festival della Creatività, Foligno

Period: September

Location: Historic center of Foligno

Uniqueness: The Festival della Creatività celebrates innovation and artistic expression through workshops, exhibitions, and performances, inviting visitors to explore the creative spirit of Umbria.

Cantine Aperte, Umbria-wide

Period: May

Location: Participating wineries across Umbria

Uniqueness: Cantine Aperte offers wine enthusiasts the opportunity to discover Umbrian's renowned wine culture, with participating wineries opening their doors for tastings, tours, and special events.

Festival delle Sagre, Trevi

Period: October

Location: Historic center of Trevi

Uniqueness: The Festival delle Sagre celebrates Umbrian culinary traditions, with local villages showcasing their specialties through food stalls, cooking demonstrations, and cultural performances.

Special Occasions

Eurochocolate, Perugia

Period: October

Location: Historic center of Perugia

Uniqueness: Eurochocolate turns Perugia into a chocolate lover's paradise, offering a delightful experience with chocolate-themed displays, tastings, and festivities.

Corsa all'Anello, Narni

Period: April

Location: Historic center of Narni

Uniqueness: Dating back to the Middle Ages, Corsa all'Anello is a historic reenactment featuring jousting tournaments, medieval parades, and colorful pageantry.

Fiera dei Morti, Perugia

Period: November

Location: Historic center of Perugia

Uniqueness: The Fiera dei Morti, or Fair of the Dead, is a centuries-old tradition where Perugia's streets come alive with market stalls, offering everything from local crafts to traditional foods.

Processione del Venerdì Santo, Assisi

Period: Good Friday

Location: Historic center of Assisi

Uniqueness: The Processione del Venerdì Santo is a solemn procession that winds through the streets of Assisi, commemorating the Passion of Christ with elaborate floats and religious icons.

Umbria in Tavola

Period: December

Location: Participating restaurants and towns across Umbria

Uniqueness: Umbria in Tavola showcases the region's culinary heritage with special menus and events hosted by restaurants and towns throughout Umbria, offering visitors a taste of traditional Umbrian cuisine.

Experience the magic of Umbrian's festivals and events, where ancient traditions and contemporary culture intertwine to create unforgettable moments in this timeless region. Join us in celebrating the spirit of Umbria!

Festival dei Due Mondi, Spoleto

Chapter 9

Road Trip from Umbria

Embarking on a road trip from Umbria opens up a world of breathtaking landscapes, charming towns, and cultural treasures. Whether you're a nature enthusiast, history buff, or culinary adventurer, hitting the road allows you to create your own itinerary and savor the journey. Here's a guide to planning an unforgettable road trip from Umbria, including tips for day trips.

Planning Your Road Trip

Choosing Your Route

Select a route that aligns with your interests and desired destinations. For a day trip, consider shorter routes like the SR2 for a scenic drive through Umbrian landscapes.

Duration and Stops

Opt for day trip itineraries with a focus on one or two key stops.

Explore towns like Assisi along the SR147 or venture to Lake Trasimeno via the SP75 for a leisurely day by the water.

Vehicle Rental and Preparation

Choose a reliable vehicle suitable for shorter journeys. Ensure your vehicle is equipped for day trips, including fuel and essentials for spontaneous stops.

Road Trip Essentials

Navigation Tools

Utilize navigation tools for day trips. Smartphone apps with real-time traffic updates are handy for navigating through shorter routes like the SR3.

Snacks and Refreshments

Pack snacks and refreshments for a day on the road. Explore local markets in towns like Perugia for on-the-go treats.

Entertainment

Create a day trip playlist and enjoy the drive. Plan visits to cultural sites or natural wonders within easy reach of Umbria.

Roadside Discoveries

Hidden Gems

Discover nearby hidden gems during day trips. The SR3 offers access to the charming town of Spello, known for its medieval architecture and floral displays.

Local Interactions

Engage with locals during day trips. Explore local markets in Gubbio or Assisi, where you can immerse yourself in the town's atmosphere.

Natural Wonders

Witness natural wonders within a day's drive. Head to the Marmore Falls via the E45 for a day surrounded by lush landscapes.

Accommodations on the Road

Charming Bed and Breakfasts

Consider B&Bs for overnight stays during longer day trips. Explore the SP298 for charming accommodations near Montefalco.

Quaint Countryside Villas

For day trips extending into the evening, look for countryside villas near the SR147, providing a tranquil retreat.

Coastal Retreats

If your day trip includes coastal views, explore seaside resorts along the SR75 for a refreshing break by the water.

Day Trip Tips

Early Start

Begin your day trip early to maximize exploration time and enjoy quiet attractions.

Flexible Itinerary

Keep your day trip itinerary flexible, allowing for spontaneous stops and discoveries.

Local Events

Check for local events or festivals happening during your day trip to add cultural experiences.

Embark on day trips from Umbria with these tips, exploring the beauty and diversity of the region and its neighboring destinations. *Buon viaggio!*

Perugia, Italy.

Chapter 10

7-Day Umbria Itinerary

Day 1: Welcome to Umbria City

Morning

- Arrive in Umbria City and check into your chosen accommodation.

- Start your day with a traditional Italian breakfast at a local café, enjoying a cappuccino and freshly baked pastries.

- Explore the historic city center, visiting landmarks like Piazza IV Novembre and Fontana Maggiore in Perugia.

Afternoon

- Lunch at a local trattoria, savoring a plate of bruschetta with tomatoes and local olive oil.

- Visit the Galleria Nazionale dell'Umbria in Perugia to immerse yourself in the region's rich art and cultural history.

Evening

- Dinner at a traditional Osteria in Perugia, indulging in a classic Umbrian dish like Pappardelle al Cinghiale (pasta with wild boar sauce).

- Take a leisurely stroll through the charming streets of Perugia, soaking in the evening ambiance.

Day 2: Exploring Historical Sites

Morning

- Breakfast with a classic cornetto and espresso.

- Visit the Basilica di San Francesco in Assisi, a UNESCO World Heritage Site, and explore its stunning frescoes.

Afternoon

- Lunch at a local enoteca in Assisi, pairing Umbrian wines with a platter of cured meats and cheeses.

- Continue exploring Assisi with a visit to Rocca Maggiore for panoramic views.

Evening

- Dinner at a restaurant overlooking the illuminated Basilica in Assisi, enjoying the enchanting atmosphere.

- Attend an evening concert or cultural event if available.

Day 3: Nature and Outdoor Activities

Morning

- Breakfast with a hearty frittata, filled with local vegetables and cheese.

- Head to Monti Sibillini National Park for a morning hike or nature walk.

Afternoon

- Picnic lunch in the park with local cheeses, cured meats, and fresh bread.

- Explore the charming town of Norcia, known for its truffles and local delicacies.

Evening

- Dinner at a local trattoria in Norcia, savoring dishes prepared with Norcia's famous black truffles.

- Relax with a post-dinner stroll through Norcia's picturesque streets.

Day 4: Culinary Delights

Morning

- Begin the day with a classic Italian breakfast.

- Participate in a cooking class in Norcia, learning to prepare traditional Umbrian dishes.

Afternoon

- Enjoy the fruits of your labor by making a delicious homemade lunch.

- Visit a local market in Norcia to purchase fresh ingredients and local products.

Evening

- Dinner at a Slow Food designated restaurant in Norcia, experiencing the best of Umbrian gastronomy.

Day 5: Relaxation and Leisure

Morning

- Leisurely breakfast with a variety of pastries and a strong espresso.

- Visit a local spa or thermal bath in Spello for relaxation.

Afternoon

- Light lunch at a spa café in Spello, with a focus on fresh salads and local, light dishes.

- Explore the picturesque town of Spello in the afternoon.

Evening

- Dinner at a cozy osteria in Spello, tasting local specialties.

- Enjoy a quiet evening in the town's serene ambiance.

Day 6: Local Art and Culture

Morning

- Breakfast featuring a variety of local jams and honey.

- Visit the Perugina Chocolate Factory in Perugia for a guided tour and chocolate tasting.

Afternoon

- Lunch at a café in Perugia, with a menu featuring chocolate-infused dishes.

- Explore the Etruscan Arch and the University of Perugia.

Evening

- Dinner at a gourmet restaurant in Perugia, concluding the meal with a chocolate dessert.

- Attend a cultural performance or art exhibition if available.

Day 7: Farewell and Departure

Morning

- Final breakfast with a selection of local pastries.

- Take a guided tour of the historic center of Todi.

Afternoon

- Lunch at a traditional Todi trattoria, savoring local specialties.

- Spend the afternoon exploring Todi's charming streets and landmarks.

Evening

- Farewell dinner at a rooftop restaurant in Todi with panoramic views.

- Departure preparations and reflections on your unforgettable Umbrian experience.

Cooking Recipes

- Day 2 Dinner: Pappardelle al Cinghiale (Wild Boar Pasta)

- Day 4 Lunch: Homemade Pizza with Fresh Ingredients

- Day 4 Dinner: Truffle Risotto

- Day 6 Lunch: Chocolate-infused Tiramisu

- Day 7 Lunch: Panzanella (Tuscan Bread Salad)

This itinerary combines the best of Umbrian culture, culinary delights, and natural beauty for an enriching and unforgettable 7-day experience. Enjoy the journey through the heart of Umbria!

Pappardelle al Cinghiale (pasta with wild boar sauce).

Chapter 11

Practical Tips for a Seamless Umbrian Experience

Safety and Emergency Information

Safety Tips

In the midst of exploring historic towns and vibrant markets, keeping an eye on personal belongings is crucial. Umbrian's popular destinations can get crowded, so vigilance is key to a worry-free journey. Additionally, respecting local traffic regulations ensures both your safety and the smooth flow of transportation.

Emergency Contacts

Understanding emergency contact information is fundamental. The universal emergency number in Italy is 112, covering police, medical, and fire services.

For specific assistance, dial 113 for the local police and 118 for medical emergencies.

It's advisable to have these numbers readily available, whether saved in your phone or written down.

Health and Safety Measures

Especially in the current global health context, following health and safety measures is paramount. Stays informed about the latest guidelines and adhere to any specific protocols in place. Carrying a compact first aid kit with essential medical supplies adds an extra layer of preparedness for unexpected situations.

Local Laws and Customs

Cultural Sensitivity

Umbria, deeply rooted in tradition, appreciates visitors who respect local customs. When exploring religious sites, dressing modestly is not only a sign of cultural sensitivity but also a requirement in some places. Greetings play a significant role in Italian culture, so mastering basic phrases like:

- "Buongiorno" (Good morning)

- "Buonasera" (Good evening)

- "Ciao" (Hello/Goodbye)... will enhance your interaction with locals.

Legal Considerations

Familiarize yourself with local laws and regulations to avoid unintentional breaches. Different regions may have specific rules, so staying informed is a mark of responsible travel. Some areas may restrict photography, especially in places of worship, so be mindful of any signage indicating such restrictions.

Tipping Etiquette

While tipping is appreciated, it's not obligatory in Italy. Rounding up the bill is a common practice, and in some restaurants, a service charge may already be included. Understanding the local tipping etiquette ensures that your gratitude is expressed appropriately.

Sustainable Travel Practices

Waste Reduction

Embrace sustainable travel practices by minimizing waste.

Using reusable water bottles and shopping bags significantly reduces single-use plastic consumption. Proper waste disposal in designated bins is a simple yet impactful contribution to the environment.

Public Transportation

Consider eco-friendly modes of travel, such as public transportation, to reduce your carbon footprint. Exploring on foot or by bicycle not only minimizes environmental impact but also allows for a more intimate experience of Umbrian's charming towns and landscapes.

Support Local

Choosing locally-owned accommodations, restaurants, and shops directly contributes to the region's economy. Purchasing souvenirs from local artisans and markets ensures that your mementos are not only meaningful but also support the thriving local craftsmanship.

Health and Medical Facilities in Umbria

Pharmacies

Locate nearby pharmacies for any over-the-counter medication needs.

It's advisable to carry a copy of essential prescriptions, ensuring smooth communication in case of language barriers.

Medical Facilities

Identify hospitals and clinics in the vicinity of your stay. While Umbria boasts a robust healthcare system, having adequate travel insurance provides an extra layer of security for unforeseen medical emergencies.

Useful Italian Phrases for Your Trip to Umbria

Mastering basic Italian phrases enhances your connection with locals. Here are additional expressions for various situations:

Greetings

- Buongiorno! - Good morning!

- Buonasera! - Good evening!

- Ciao! - Hello/Hi/Goodbye!

- Salve! - Hello/Hi (more formal)

Common Courtesies

- Per favore - Please

- Grazie - Thank you

- Prego - You're welcome

- Scusa/Scusami - Excuse me (formal/informal)

Polite Phrases

- Mi dispiace - I'm sorry

- Permesso? - May I? /Excuse me?

- Con permesso - Excuse me (when moving through a crowded space)

Basic Conversation

- Come stai? - How are you? (Informal)

- Come sta? - How are you? (Formal)

- Sto bene, grazie - I'm fine, thank you

- Molto bene - Very well

Navigating

- "Come si arriva a...?" (How do I get to...?)

- "Posso avere il menu?" (Can I have the menu?)

- "Dove si trova il bagno?" (Where is the bathroom?)

Asking for Information

- Dov'è...? - Where is...?

- Quanto costa? - How much does it cost?

- Parla inglese? - Do you speak English?

Numbers and Directions

- Uno, due, tre - One, two, three

- A sinistra - To the left

- A destra - To the right

Emergencies

- Aiuto! - Help!

- Chiamate un'ambulanza! - Call an ambulance!

- Ho bisogno di aiuto. - I need help.

- Sono perso/a. - I'm lost.

Farewells

- Arrivederci - Goodbye (formal)

- Addio - Farewell (more formal or permanent)

- A presto - See you soon

- Ciao ciao! - Bye bye! (Informal)

Feel free to use these phrases to enhance your interactions during your trip to Umbria!

Conclusion

As we conclude this travel guide to **Umbria in 2025**, I am filled with gratitude for the opportunity to guide you through this mesmerizing region. Umbria, often referred to as the "**Green Heart of Italy**," has unfolded its treasures before you—a kaleidoscope of medieval towns, rolling vineyards, and historic wonders. Crafting this travel guide has been a journey of discovery, an exploration of the hidden gems and vibrant traditions that make Umbria a destination like no other.

From the bustling markets of **Perugia** to the serene shores of **Lake Trasimeno**, every corner of Umbria beckons with its own unique charm. The warmth of the locals, the flavors of traditional cuisine, and the timeless beauty of historical sites all converge to create an experience that lingers in the heart.

I extend my heartfelt thanks for choosing this guide as your companion on your journey through Umbria. Your exploration of this captivating region is a testament to the spirit of adventure and a curiosity for the world's wonders. As you savor the delights of Umbria, may each moment be a celebration of culture, history, and the simple joys of travel.

For more travel adventures and guides, I invite you to explore my collection of books and also leave your testimonials under this book in Amazon store. Your support is a source of inspiration, and I look forward to bringing you more tales from around the globe. Until then, may your travels be filled with joy, discovery, and the magic that Umbria has graciously shared with me.

Grazie mille and happy travels!

Printed in Dunstable, United Kingdom